On the Banks of

BIG ELK CREEK

On the Banks of
BIG ELK CREEK

The Life of Martha Finley
Beloved Author of The Elsie Books

BARBARA ZAHN

WITH NANCY DRAZGA

FULL
QUART
PRESS

An Imprint of
Holly Hall Publications, Inc.

On the Banks of Big Elk Creek
The Life of Martha Finley—Beloved Author of The Elsie Books

by Barbara Zahn with Nancy Drazga

© 1997 by Barbara Zahn and Nancy Drazga
ISBN 1-888306-19-X

Published by Holly Hall Publications
255 South Bridge Street
P.O. Box 254
Elkton, MD 21922-0254
Tel. (410) 392-5554

Send requests for information to the above address.

Cover & book design by Mark Dinsmore
Arkworks@aol.com

Printed in the United States of America.

Preface

IF A WRITER'S WORLDVIEW can be ascertained from her writings, we can say without doubt that Martha Finley was deeply devout, that she was a woman who saw God's hand in everything, and that she had a deep-felt desire to lay before her readers how to reach a saving knowledge of Jesus Christ. She was as quick to see the humor in a situation as she was to feel compassion for those in tragic circumstances; her sense of Christian charity knew no bounds. She had a contempt for selfish and unmannerly behavior and a hatred for immorality and the evil that men do.

There is a great deal that we do not know about the life of the woman who became famous in her day as the creator of Elsie Dinsmore, the beautiful Southern heiress who was a household word in the last decades of the nineteenth century and well into the twentieth century. We have tried to fill in the gaps in the record with what "could have happened," based on what we know of Elsie's life and character, and what we can surmise from our reading of her books—particularly the Mildred series, which are thought to be autobiographical.

On the Banks of Big Elk Creek, therefore, is biographical fiction. Hopefully, we have used what is known about Martha Finley to give you a believable picture of a woman who was without doubt talented, high-spirited, inquisitive, independent, loyal, sentimental, and faithful to her God. She was well-read in the classics as well as the literature of her day, and she was a great student of the Bible. As a writer, she was indefatigable: she produced some fifty novels—and innumerable short stories—most of which were written without the aid of a typewriter (much less a computer!).

For those of you who want to know what in our story is true, beyond the public records of her birth and death, we know that she lost her mother early in life and that her physician father remarried and moved to South Bend, Indiana. Martha did go east to school, and malaria did strike the town of South Bend. She did become a schoolteacher after the death of her father. And of course we know about her writing, because it was published—although certain family members were less than thrilled about that!

In the 1870's she moved to Elkton, Maryland—where her stepmother and her brother Charles and his family resided—and built the big house that still stands at 259 East Main Street. We know from her will that she died a wealthy woman. Interested fans will find a large monument at the site of her grave in Elkton's cemetery. Also, the Cecil County Historical Society has an exhibit displaying some of Martha Finley's original books and possessions. The Elkton Library, in Elkton, Maryland, has a large collection of the original Elsie Dinsmore books.

We hope you enjoy reading our story of Martha Finley as much as we have enjoyed writing it! Happy reading!

—Barbara Zahn and Nancy Drazga

Chapter One

MARTHA'S WORLD

THE FINLEYS WERE IN A HURRY. "Martha, please make every minute count," called Mama from the hallway. "We don't want to be late for the parade."

In the blue and white bedroom she shared with an older sister, ten-year-old Martha was lying on her bed reading a book—her third one that week. Stretched out on her stomach, feet in the air, dressed only in her camisole and pantalettes, she was completely absorbed in the story, eager to see what would happen next. So engrossed was she that she didn't hear her stepmother's admonition.

"Martha, what are you doing? You are far from ready! Goodness, child, put down that book and get into your dress!" Her stepmother frowned as she entered the room.

The youngest Finley daughter at once jumped up and quickly slipped into her new red dress. "Thank goodness this dress doesn't have as many buttons as some of my other ones," she thought to herself. As she stood in front of the full-length mirror, the image that looked back at her was that of a petite girl with fine, brown, shoulder-length hair, streaked blond by the sun, a round, smooth face, a small mouth, and deep, inquisitive brown eyes. Combing her hair, she tried to arrange a troublesome curl that wanted to have its own way.

"Oh, Mama," she sighed, "what can I do with my hair? This curl just won't stay in place. See, it sticks out." With a furrowed brow displacing her usually sunny face, she complained, "I can't be ready on time—and besides, everyone will laugh at me when I do get there."

"Well, dear, I really don't think most people will even notice," her stepmother said gently. "All eyes will be on the parade. You know, no one cares about anything else when there is a little excitement in town. Why don't you wear your wide-brim hat with the crisp ruffle? It will keep that troublesome curl in place," she said, handing Martha the hat, adding, "and keep the hot sun off your face as well. But don't delay any longer—we really should be going."

Martha thought her stepmother was always in a hurry—leaving behind her a faint scent of lemon cologne everywhere she passed, her long skirts rustling about her ankles. But she would have been the first to admit that the household ran smoothly under Mary Finley's management. Martha reflected that her small-boned, refined stepmother hurried with a certain elegance, and usually there was a pleasant smile upon her fine, delicate face. And today, Martha thought, she looked even more elegant than usual. Mrs. Finley was dressed in a full-skirted light blue cotton gown trimmed with lace at the bosom and sleeves. Her eyes were a blue-grey that seemed to change depending upon the mood she was in or the color of her dress—and today in her blue gown they were decidedly blue. Her thick dark brown hair was parted in the middle and combed back into two heavy braids that she had twined around her head, leaving a few wisps of curls to frame her face.

Martha tried on the bonnet. "Very becoming," said Mrs. Finley. "Here, let's put this bow on the side. It perfectly matches the color of your new dress."

Martha looked in the mirror again. This time her reflection showed the small girl with a smiling face and cheeks flushed with pleasure.

"See how pretty you look!" said her stepmother proudly. "Your bonnet bow really sets off the red print in your dress, and the red sash, and that high waist really suits you. Just be careful as we walk down the street that you don't get your white shoes soiled. My, what a lovely picture you make!"

Ready at last, Martha gave one last longing look at the book she had left lying on the bed and closed the door. Part of her wished she could stay home so she could find out what was going to happen to the heroine in the story, but the other part of her was eager to see the parade, and her father dressed in all his Scottish finery.

Dr. James Finley was also getting dressed, and he, too, was full of anticipation. When Martha and his wife knocked on his dressing room door, he had just pulled on his plaid knee socks and was fretting about whether he had all the pieces of his Scottish costume.

"Come in," he called. "I could use some help from the two of you," he added, as they entered the large, airy room. A gentle breeze was playing with the starched white curtains at the open windows.

After admiring their gowns, he asked, "What do you think of my finery? Will I be acceptable? And shall I wink as I go by, daughter?" His family were eager spectators of this early fall event, but Dr. Finley was actually one of the participants. One of only three men in the small but thriving town of South Bend, Indiana, who could play the bagpipes, he was quite proud of his mastery of Scotland's national instrument.

"Oh yes, Papa. Do wink at us! I promise I'll wave," Martha responded. "You know, I think your kilt is the prettiest of all the plaids. Don't you like all the colors in it, Mama?"

"Yes, I do. His plaid is one of my favorites, also. But, of course," she said, her eyes twinkling, "it might have something to do with who is wearing it! But remember, the proper name for that design is 'tartan,' Martha. As a young lady of Scotch-Irish descent, you must know these things."

"What big knees you have, Papa!" said his daughter with a giggle. "I guess your socks won't cover them!" Changing the subject, she exclaimed, "I wish girls could wear the kilts and march. Men and boys have all the fun. Someday I'm going to do fun things, too!" And a small sigh escaped her lips.

"Martha, help me with the other parts of your father's costume," her mother urged. "It's getting late. We must be ready to go in a few minutes." Glancing around, Mrs. Finley asked, "Where's the sporran? Now, Martha, do you remember where it goes? Yes, that's right, in front of the kilt. Now, get the doublet and bonnet from the chair over there and give them to your father."

Martha hastened to obey, and soon her father was ready. He was a tall man who carried himself with distinction, and today, dressed in his Scottish costume, he looked quite the man of nobility.

Martha said proudly, "Oh, Papa, you are so handsome! I like the Finley sett better than all the others I saw last year."

"Hmmm, I seem to be missing something, daughter. Do you know where my brogues are? A gentleman cannot be well-dressed without his shoes," Dr. Finley reminded her with a rueful grin.

"Oh, here they are—under the bed!" exclaimed Martha. "See how shiny they are! Mama did a good job of polishing them last night, didn't she?" said Martha, as she handed him the shoes.

"She certainly did," he agreed, putting them on. "Now, let me put on my tartan, and get it fastened over my shoulder with the brooch, and I shall be ready to go. Where are Samuel and the girls? Tell them we're ready, and let's be off," he said, escorting them from the room with a flourish. He, too, was eager to get started.

The Finleys lived at the edge of town, and they made quite a parade themselves as they walked to the field on which the parade and other festivities were to be held on this early fall day in 1838. There were seven Finleys in all: the doctor and his wife, Samuel, Mary, Eleanor, Elizabeth, and Martha, the youngest. The Finleys, as well as the other residents of the town, were looking forward to the parade of the Scottish highlanders dressed in their kilts and plaids, and the hours of fun and games that were to follow. The gathering today was not expected to be large—nothing like the Independence Day parade in July—but it had grown larger every year, and all who had attended in earlier years had enjoyed themselves very much.

The day was mild and pleasant. The very faint touch of autumn color in the trees was the only hint of cooler days ahead. Birds were singing, preparing for their fall migration, bees were making their last rounds before retiring to their hives for the winter, and a squirrel chattered a warning when they passed too near his tree. The fields were aglow with golden rod, daisies, blue bellflowers, and Queen Anne's lace. Mary, Eleanor, and Elizabeth picked a bouquet, putting some of the blooms in their hair. Samuel, leaping a small roadside ditch, said he wanted nothing to do with the flowers, because they made him sneeze. At this, of course, the sisters playfully stuck the bouquets under his nose.

"What a perfect day for a gathering, before the weather turns cold," remarked Mrs. Finley. "I am looking forward to making a pumpkin pie. Our pumpkins are almost ready."

"My mouth is watering at the very thought, my dear," said her husband with a genial smile.

Martha spoke up. "Papa," she asked, "what if you lose your cap? Remember what happened to Mr. MacTavish last year when he tripped?" Giggling at the memory, she continued, "His cap tilted to the side and he could hardly play the bagpipes. Remember how the crowd laughed, Mama? And remember the year before, when Mr. MacGregor's bagpipes got stuck and made all those weird sounds, and all the babies started crying?"

Dr. Finley and his wife smiled as they listened to their daughter chattering away like a magpie.

"Oh, Papa, I would be so embarrassed if anything like that happened to you. But it would be funny. What if your sporran fell off right in the middle of the street? Whatever would you do?" she asked suddenly, side-stepping a puddle.

Martha's older sister Mary, arranging her bouquet with the expertise of one long practiced at such things, spoke up from behind. "Martha, you are such a chatterbox! Why don't you pick some flowers?"

"Yes, really, Martha, enough of this," chided her father. "You have such an imagination! Let's trust God that none of these unfortunate accidents will befall your 'poor old papa' today." Giving Mrs. Finley a look of amusement, he rolled his eyes heavenward.

Just then, Elizabeth laughed, and exclaimed, "Look at Samuel!" As they turned to look at him, one by one they too began to laugh.

Samuel's face turned a bright pink. "What are you all laughing about?" he asked hotly.

"Look at your socks, and you will see," said Eleanor, between laughs.

Samuel, in his forays off the path, had managed to get into some "stick-tights"—brown burrs that grew along roadsides and attached themselves to fur, clothing, or almost any other substance that came into contact with them. They were all over his socks and trousers, some even clinging to his shirt.

"Oh, Samuel," Martha giggled, "you look so funny!"

Dr. Finley, however, noting his son's embarrassment, came to his rescue, and between the two of them, they plucked them all off, and Samuel's dignity was restored.

When they reached the parade field a few moments later, Dr. Finley bade his family farewell as he joined his friends. Martha called, "Don't forget to wink, Papa! We'll wave back at you!"

It was a day of excitement for everyone in South Bend, whether of Scottish descent or not. There were foot races and relay races, dancing, and bagpipe music. Spectators cheered on the participants, children ran to and fro, and neighbors waved and greeted one another. The favorite game of all was tossing the "caber." As the caber was a long wooden pole weighing about 180 pounds, the game was quite a test of strength. Samuel was planning to compete this year, and the family was eager to see how far he could throw the pole. Martha, her worries of the morning forgotten, found herself having a delightful time. She and her sisters thought the food was even better than it had been the year before. But all too soon it was time to go home.

Lying snugly in bed that night, underneath the light blanket, Martha reminisced about her day. She thought about the food, the games, the music, the chats with friends, and all the beautiful tartan plaids she had seen. She concluded again that her father's was the most colorful of all. Still not happy with the tradition that only men and boys could wear the kilts and play the pipes, she wondered if there was anything she could do about it. She was still wondering as she fell fast asleep.

* * * * * *

Martha Finley was born in Chillicothe, Ohio, on April 26, 1828, in the home of her grandfather, Major Samuel Finley, of the Virginia Cavalry. She was the sixth child of Lieutenant James and Maria Finley, both natives of Pennsylvania. Her mother died when she was very young, and her father moved his family to Philadelphia, where he received the family's help in raising his children. It was in Philadelphia that he was subsequently remarried to a fine Christian woman, whom the children soon learned to call mama.

When Martha was around eight years old, James and his second wife, Mary, moved with the children to the small rural town of South Bend, Indiana, not far from Lake Michigan. Here Dr. Finley set up a medical practice, and the family settled into the life of the small prairie town.

Their children's education was a great concern to Dr. and Mrs. Finley. In their correspondence with relatives back in Philadelphia they discussed the possibility of two of the girls spending a year back East. Finally, Mary, who was eighteen years old, and Martha, who was now eleven, were chosen. They felt that Martha, bookish and precocious, would benefit from a better education than the resources a frontier town could provide, and Mary, they knew, would enjoy Philadelphia society. Samuel, Eleanor, and Elizabeth were not the least bit happy about not being allowed to go.

Preparations were made for a journey by stagecoach, not the smoothest means of travel, but the most expedient under the circumstances. Two daughters traveling without an escort was a frightening thought to their parents, but Martha thought it a great adventure.

Soon the day of departure arrived. Martha was aglow with anticipation. Mary tried to be a little more sedate and dignified, as she thought befitted her age, but she, too, was excited about the journey. Their Saratoga trunks carefully packed and their shoes polished, the girls dressed warmly and put on their prettiest bonnets. The whole family, except Samuel, went in the carriage with them to the station to see them off. Samuel followed in the wagon that carried their trunks.

A very anxious Mrs. Finley repeatedly admonished her daughters, "Don't make friends with any gentlemen, don't grumble, and walk when the driver tells you to, because you will need the exercise. Don't complain about the food at the stop stations, and pray for God's grace to get you there."

She went on, "Do expect discomfort, annoyance, and disappointment, because you will surely get them." Then she turned to her husband and said, "James, I think this whole trip should be called off. I am just so afraid for them to go alone. Why did we ever decide to do this, anyway?"

"Kiss them good-bye, my dear. The coach is ready to leave," he gently said, turning aside and unobtrusively brushing away the tears from his eyes. He, too, would sorely miss his daughters, but he knew the decision to let them go had been a good one. He especially wanted Martha to have an opportunity to attend a good school where both the teachers and the material would challenge her. Martha was his little scholar, and he hoped very much that she would make good use of her time in Philadelphia.

The other passengers on the eastbound coach were two gentlemen and a mother and her two children. Mrs. Finley was quite relieved when she saw the older woman in the traveling party.

Waving good-bye to their family, the girls settled back on straight hard-cushioned seats, which, they realized almost immediately, promised to be very uncomfortable. Following the well-known National Road, which ran from Ohio to Philadelphia, Baltimore, and Washington, D. C., the stagecoach bounced along at the brisk speed of ten miles per hour. The trip to Philadelphia would take three long days. As the stagecoach ran day and night, with only ten-minute stops for changing horses, quick meals, and brief stretches, they were very grateful for the picnic basket their stepmother had handed in to them just before the coach departed. Packed full to the brim, its contents would do much to make the journey bearable.

Very little sleep was possible, and by journey's end they were tired and stiff, and their traveling clothes were very limp and rumpled.

"Oh, how completely right mother was!" Mary groaned to Martha, stretching her weary body during one of the brief stops.

"I know," responded Martha. "I think I'll never stop aching from all the bumps and jolts."

At their journey's end they were met by their relatives in Philadelphia and whisked away to their lovely home and a well-needed rest. Happy that the rigors of travel were behind them, the sisters fell quickly asleep on the soft, cozy feather beds in the airy second-floor bedroom that was to be theirs for the next year.

After they were fully rested, the sisters were taken by carriage to view the sights of Philadelphia. Asked what they thought of the "City of Brotherly Love," Martha exclaimed, "It's so big and noisy! There are horses and carts and coaches everywhere. There is no order in the streets—it's all one big traffic jam!"

Mary agreed that it was certainly different from the small town in Indiana that they had left behind. Neither of them liked the garbage in the street or the sooty smoke of the factories.

"The smell is so horrible that one must hold a scented handkerchief over one's nose, and there are so many row houses—they look like books on a shelf. It's a wonder people can bear to live in them!" Mary stated emphatically.

Philadelphia was an important American city at this time. It was the home of the Liberty Bell and Independence Hall—the building in which the Declaration of Independence was signed and the Constitution was drafted. Both Mary and Martha enjoyed visiting these historic sites, and were proud to call themselves Americans.

During the period of 1839-40, Martha was enrolled in a private school, where she was drilled in her sums—using an abacus—and also her grammar. Much recitation and composition were required for her history and religion courses, and she spent much time reading and preparing for her classes. She enjoyed her classes in music and drawing most of all, and was also able to spend some of her time knitting and sewing. Mary spent her time visiting with relatives and attending society functions with her cousins and their parents.

At the end of Martha's school year, they reluctantly returned to their home in South Bend, Indiana. It seemed to both girls that the year had gone by far too quickly. Martha found it especially difficult to return to a rural schoolhouse after her classes in the private school in Philadelphia.

Chapter Two

A CARRIAGE RIDE TO CHURCH

IT WAS A WARM, clear Sunday morning. Riding along to church, the Finley family enjoyed the soft, gentle breeze and the clear blue sky. Dr. Finley held the reins lightly as their faithful horse pulled the shiny black carriage— its fine gold stripe glittering in the sun—along the dusty street. Molly the horse seemed to know her way very well to the First Presbyterian Church of South Bend.

Martha and one-year-old Amy were squeezed between their parents on the front seat of the open carriage. With one arm, Mrs. Finley was carefully holding newborn Theresa on her lap—the other was around Amy's waist. Samuel, Eleanor, and Elizabeth were sitting in the back seat, watching the passersby as the carriage made its way to the church. Mary was suffering from a cold and had stayed at home.

Eleanor and Elizabeth had recently received new bonnets, and were very happy to be able to display them in the new open carriage. Eleanor's bonnet, a deep blue with matching lace and a ribbon that tied under the chin, perfectly matched her blue gown and her blue eyes. Elizabeth's was pink silk and matched the pink ruffles and pink stitching on her white gown. Placing one perfectly gloved hand on the bonnet and fingering the pink feather to be sure it had not blown away, with the other hand she waved to friends they passed on the street. She looked as pretty as a picture, and she was well aware of the fact.

Samuel thought his sisters were making too much out of a trip to church. As far as he was concerned, his "Sunday-go-to-meeting" clothes—brown knee breeches and cream-colored shirt—were quite sufficient. Ladies' fashions did not interest him at all, and he had told his sisters every time he got the chance that he was tired of stepping over wide skirts with dozens of petticoats underneath, just to be able to get into the carriage. Of course, his sisters ignored all his comments about the inconvenience of women's fashions.

"Those clouds look just like cotton candy hanging in the sky!" exclaimed Mrs. Finley. "What a beautiful Sabbath! The sun is very bright, though," she commented. "Girls, do be careful today, that you don't get burned. It's bad for your skin, and it will ruin your complexion. Young ladies must not allow their complexions to become brown from the sun!" With that admonition, she sat back to enjoy the ride.

"Papa," spoke Eleanor from the back, "why didn't you get some gold scrolling on the carriage? It is quite the thing, you know, and it would have perfectly matched the gold stripe."

Her father laughed. "My dear girl," he chided, "if you knew how much this vehicle cost, you would be quite thankful to be riding in it without the scrolling. I'm afraid my pocketbook just couldn't afford any more. Doctors are not rich, you know. What do you think of the corduroy upholstery? Does that suit your fancy?" They all joined in the conversation, and after some discussion of the decor of the new carriage,

Samuel conceded that he wished the upholstery could have been leather, even though he did like the maroon color of the corduroy. Martha, not interested in the discussion of the various options available for the carriage, was off in her own world.

Suddenly, as though the carriage had jolted her back into the present, suddenly the ever-inquisitive young lady asked, "Why do we go to this church? We just passed a Lutheran church and a Baptist church. Over on the next street is a Methodist church—I see its steeple from here. Why have we always gone to the Presbyterian church?" She looked up at her father, who seemed to be intently studying the reins he held in his hand.

Dr. Finley sighed. His wife smiled. He often called Martha his "little question box with no lid," and declared that he could never satisfy all she wanted to know. "She has such an active mind," he mused. "She is always asking questions—always thinking things over."

From the back of the carriage Eleanor muttered, "Oh no, here we go again." Samuel simply groaned.

"Well, daughter," he began, "as you know, the Finleys are of Scotch-Irish descent, and the Presbyterian church is the official Scottish church. We feel it is where the Lord would have our family worship." Then addressing all the children, he added, "The great thing about America is that people may worship God in whatever church they choose. We go to the Presbyterian church because most of our family has gone there through the years. You know, there have been quite a few Presbyterian preachers in our family," he added with pride.

"Will we ever go to another church?" asked Elizabeth, from the back seat.

Mrs. Finley smiled again. She enjoyed listening to her husband's responses to the children's questions.

"He always seems to know what to say," she thought to herself.

"We may, someday," answered Dr. Finley. "There are many great Bible preachers and teachers in other churches. Jonathan Blanchard is in the Congregationalist church and is working hard for the Lord. I have heard wonderful reports of his ministry. Many people are coming to Christ through his efforts."

There was a pause, and then Mrs. Finley said, "Children, there is a scripture verse in the book of Hebrews that encourages us to join together in one place to worship God. The word used is 'assemble,' and that place is the church. We are to come together to encourage each other." She looked around at all of them. "It is a good thing to help one another. Even in our home, we should all encourage each other to be obedient to God."

Martha asked, "What kind of church does George Mueller attend? Mrs. Hanks, my Sunday school teacher, calls him 'the man who gets things from God.' "

"I believe he comes from a Lutheran and Brethren background. He's doing a great work among the homeless children," replied her father.

"Yes, Mrs. Hanks told us how he feeds all those orphans. She said there are hundreds of them! Someday I'm going to tell that story!" Martha's eyes sparkled as she thought about it.

"Martha," cautioned her stepmother, "the most important thing to remember is to love God. We must all be sure we have accepted Jesus into our hearts and repented of our sins, as the Bible instructs. This is what is most important of all—much more important than which church we go to."

As they neared the church, the horse slowed to a walk. Samuel was eager to disembark. He was tired of listening to his younger sister's questions.

Martha wiggled in her seat, as impatient as Samuel, though for a different reason. She just couldn't be still—she had so many questions, and never enough time to ask them all.

"Why don't we read the newspaper on Sunday, Papa? Why may we read only our Bibles or some religious material?"

"My, my, what a barrage of questions today!" responded Dr. Finley. "This is the day we set aside as the Lord's day, and I believe Sunday's reading should be from God's words, rather than from man's."

"Why don't we play cards?" was Martha's next question. "Some of my friends do."

The two adults exchanged glances, amused but somewhat in awe of their little daughter's great thirst for information. Samuel and Elizabeth simply groaned. "Ah, here we are at the church," said Dr. Finley, a little glad for the respite. "Enough questions for one carriage ride, I should think."

Stopping the carriage, he disembarked and tethered the horse. Then going around to the other side of the carriage, he handed down first his wife, and then his daughters, saying as he did so, "Watch your step, now, ladies. There you go. Eleanor, please help your mother with the baby. Elizabeth, you take Amy's hand, or pick her up if she won't walk. Samuel, please escort your sister Martha. I'll be along in a moment."

* * * * * * *

"Hurry, hurry, hurry," thought Martha to herself. She wished the minister would finish his sermon. The seat of the pew was hard, its back was too straight, and the choir had been uninspiring. Besides, there was so much she wanted to think about. It was hard to keep her mind on the sermon, but she knew her father would be displeased if he noticed that she wasn't paying attention. She saw a sunbeam dancing on the stained glass window near their pew and watched it as it made the colors in the glass glitter and twinkle. Glancing over at Samuel, she saw that his eyes were closed and knew he was sleeping in church again. Her father apparently hadn't noticed. The preacher went on and on, and in spite of her best efforts, her thoughts wandered. Weren't there women who were well known for serving God? Hadn't she heard of an invalid lady who wrote hymns? Yes, her name was Charlotte Elliott. She remembered that Miss Elliott had written many songs. She especially loved a particular one her mother hummed as she went about her work. It was called, "Just As I Am."

Eleanor nudged her. She looked over quickly at her father, and then looked straight ahead. She tried once again to concentrate on the minister's words, but soon her thoughts were again far away. She remembered her mama telling her that Miss Elliott often endured times of grave suffering.

"Hurry, hurry, hurry," she whispered to herself, impatient for the minister to finish. She wanted to ask about Charlotte Elliott on the carriage ride home.

Chapter Three

GROWING UP

"OH, CARRIE, WHAT A WONDERFUL PARTY! I can't believe I'm sixteen years old!" exclaimed Martha to her best friend.

"Yes, it was lovely, wasn't it?" responded Carrie, with a smile. "And those little sandwiches your mother made were wonderful! Let's go sit in the garden until my mother comes for me," she suggested.

Martha acquiesced, glad for a few moments of quiet repose after the excitement of the party. The two girls seated themselves on a low bench near the small fountain, from which a glistening shower of water was gushing and then raining lightly down onto the bright pebbles that lined the small pool. The minnows in the pool were darting about like twinkling jewels. Nearby were large flower beds, which would soon be filled with the blooms of the perennials that provided color and fragrance throughout the spring and summer. The crocuses were up, and the daffodils. The large patch of wild violets—Martha's favorite flowers—were beginning to bloom. Above their seat a cherry tree was in full bloom, its blossoms perfuming the air around them. This was a favorite spot of the whole family, who enjoyed relaxing in the pastoral setting, watching the dancing water of the fountain and listening to the many birds that had made the garden their home. No one enjoyed it more than Dr. Finley, who found it a perfect place to unwind after a long day of taking care of his sick patients. The early evening breeze felt good on their glowing faces, which were flushed with the excitement of the day.

"It certainly is lovely out here," commented Martha. "Today was unusually hot for April. I'm glad Mama let me take off a few of my petticoats after the others left. I guess I'm more interested in comfort than fashion!"

Looking up at the beautiful pink flowers of the cherry tree, she added, "But I shouldn't be complaining about my petticoats! Tonight, in my diary I will write: 'April 26, 1844. Today I celebrated my sixteenth birthday. Mama and Papa gave me a wonderful party, and all my friends came. It was a perfect day.' "

Carrie laughed. "It was indeed," she said, "and we're all very glad you enjoyed it so much."

"I did, immensely, and I'm also very grateful for all the help you gave Mama, for I know you helped her plan it!" Martha jumped up and made a low curtsy to her friend. Then sitting down and sighing pensively, she said, "Carrie, I do wonder what God has in store for me. I don't think I'll ever finish school, and all Mama and Papa talk about is how we children must get a good education so we can support ourselves when we get older. That's why they sent me back East to school a few years ago—so I could get a better educational foundation."

"Well, in just a few more years we'll be women of the world, as they say. We'll get married, and soon after that, we'll have a houseful of babies," laughed Carrie. "Sometimes I can't wait to be grown up, and sometimes I want to stay a child forever."

Although Carrie was a year older than she was, Martha could almost picture Carrie as a "child forever." She was bubbly and gay, never in a hurry, and was always nonchalant and free in her manner—qualities very endearing in a child, but ones that had caused her mother many an anxious moment as her daughter grew into a young lady. Carrie, with her long dark hair, blue eyes and long lashes, had always been pretty, but she was fast becoming a beauty.

Pushing back her fine hair from her face, and re-tying the bow of her pink hair ribbon, Martha replied, "Yes, Carrie, our childhood will be gone before we realize it. And you will probably be married in a few years, as pretty as you are. You already have two or three beaux. But not I. In fact, I wonder if I'm ever going to look like a—a—" She paused.

"A what?" urged her friend.

"Well, you know, like a lady. Look at me! I'm little, and papa says he doesn't think I'm going to get much taller. He says I take after his younger sister, Auntie Ruth. I'll probably always look like a little girl," she said despairingly. "I wish I were taller, like my sisters. Mama says I shouldn't talk about such things. She says I should 'let nature take its course,' as she calls it."

Ready for a change of subject, Carrie asked, "Speaking of petticoats, how many do you think Mrs. Murray had under her gown today? I've never seen such a full skirt. I don't know how she even managed to sit down."

Giggling, Martha said, "I know what you mean! She looked like a stuffed pillow. And all those ruffles! She certainly has a small waist, though—smaller than mine, I think. And she's old—all or more of thirty, isn't she?" she said, grimacing at the thought of anyone being that old.

"Probably," answered Carrie. "I'm not sure. But you're right, her waist is probably not more than twenty inches around. Her corset must have been pulled so tight she could hardly breathe!"

"I guess there's some advantage after all to being so small," grinned Martha. "I would hate to be laced up that tight! Being fashionable can be so uncomfortable. Whoever thought of women wearing all this understuff anyway? And ruffles—I guess if the sewing machine hadn't been invented, we wouldn't have to worry about all this ruffly stuff, would we? Somebody told me that with a sewing machine you can stitch a whole seam in the blink of an eye. I'd like to see that!" she laughed. "I think we should blame the senselessness of women's fashions on the man who invented the sewing machine! Don't you think that's a good idea?"

"Oh, Martha, you are so funny," responded Carrie, with a laugh. "Despite your love of books, and all that reading you do, you still have such a silly sense of humor. Sometimes I think you could be funny and get paid for it—if it were a proper thing for a lady to do. But since you can't join a circus, you'll probably get married or end up being a 'school marm,' and telling silly stories to your children or your students."

Martha looked at her feet, wondering what it would be like to join a circus, and thinking how nice it would be to take off her shoes and socks and dip her feet into the pool. "And I will probably end up being a school teacher," she said with a little frown, "as I just don't see marriage in my future. And I've certainly gone to school long enough to qualify as a teacher."

"That's certainly true," said Carrie, who sometimes wished she were as intelligent and curious about things as Martha was. She knew Martha made excellent grades, and she couldn't count the times Martha had earned the teacher's highest grade—the "Reward of Merit." Carrie had never known her friend to be late for class or tardy with an assignment. Martha was already well read in history, and Carrie imagined that by the time she was twenty she would have read every book her father could buy. Though Martha's standard of right was much higher than hers, Carrie was glad that they were friends—they had even dubbed themselves "friends for life."

Martha was thinking about her birthday celebration again. "The party was wonderful," she reiterated, "but I wish some of my relatives from Pennsylvania and Maryland could have been here. It would have made Mama and Papa so happy."

"Yes," agreed Carrie, "but your family is so large now—with your older brother and sisters, and all the younger ones, too. Where would you have put them? I know your house is large, but it is already filled to overflowing with all the people who are living in it now."

Martha laughed happily. "Yes, I know, Carrie. There are a lot of us, but we seem to make out all right, and we would have tucked the relatives into various nooks and crannies. Besides, there's a little more room than you think, because two of my older sisters are on their own now.

"You see, Carrie," she continued, "the family is very important to Mama and Papa. They want us to spend time with our aunts and uncles and cousins whenever possible, and birthdays and holidays are perfect occasions for getting together. Mama and Papa want us to know who our relatives are—those who are living as well as those who have passed on!" she finished, with a grin.

"What do you mean by that?" asked Carrie, a little confused.

"Oh, many of my relatives went to university and were leaders of the country. My parents are forever talking about them. I guess they are really proud of them. Papa says we have two relatives who are really famous!" As she spoke, Martha laughed, placed her hand over her heart, and gave Carrie a mischievous look.

"Who are they?" queried Carrie. "Have I ever met them?"

Giggling, Martha said, "No silly, they've been dead for years. My grandfather, General Samuel Finley, was a major in the War of 1812. He was nicknamed 'Brave Little Major,' and he was a personal friend of George Washington. Washington even appointed him collector of public monies in the Northwestern Territory, which is what took him to Ohio. You know, he was one of its early settlers. Can you imagine—a personal friend of the president?" Martha grew serious. "You know, Carrie, that would be like you and me being friends with President Tyler right now!"

"Goodness!" exclaimed Carrie, her eyes widening at the thought. "You're right. Just think, what if we actually got invited to the Presidential Palace in Washington, D. C. They say it has all kinds of rooms—the Red Room, the Blue Room, the Green Room—"

"That's not all either," interrupted Martha. "There's a State Dining Room, an East Room, a China Room, and others I can't remember the names of. We learned about them in history session. Do you know anyone who has ever been there?"

"No, but I wish I did. I'd like to ask him what it's really like," said Carrie.

"Me too. I'd have a lot of questions. I've heard that on the second floor there are all kinds of rooms too."

"Where does the Tyler family sleep?" asked Carrie.

"According to my information," intoned Martha in her best imitation-school-teacher-voice, "the presidential family has their own private living quarters on the second floor." In her normal voice, she said wistfully, "I guess it must be really grand."

She paused, imagining what it would be like to live in such a place, then continued, saying to Carrie, "Did you know that the entire mansion was burned by the

British during the War of 1812? That's not so long ago—only thirty-two years."

"Oh yes, I know all about that. President James Madison and his wife, Dolley, were forced to run for their lives. She wouldn't leave until she had taken down the large portrait of George Washington, because she didn't want to leave it behind for the British to destroy. See Miss Martha, I know some history, too." Carrie laughed and tapped her friend gently on the head.

"Well, thank goodness, it's all over, and the mansion has been repaired," said Martha, smoothing her long skirt and pushing back her hair again. "One thing I really like about Dolley Madison," she added, irrelevantly, "is that she was short—just like me, and just like Zacchaeus in the Bible."

Carrie removed her shoes and stockings and dipped her toes in the pool. Happy that she no longer needed to keep up appearances, Martha did the same. Continuing their discussion, Carrie said, "I wonder why the name of the president's home has been changed so many times. In 1818, it was named the Executive Mansion. Since then it has been given three other names: the President's Mansion, the President's Home, and now, the President's Palace. My teacher said it has now been painted white—to cover up the scorch marks left by the British cannons."

"That is right," said Martha, "and imagine how impressive it must look! It stands in the middle of a beautiful eighteen-acre plot of land on Pennsylvania Avenue. Wouldn't you just love to see it? I think it would be so exciting!" she exclaimed.

"Who was the other famous Finley ancestor?" questioned Carrie.

"Oh, that was my great-uncle, Samuel Finley. He was a minister, and became president of Princeton Theological Seminary in New Jersey. According to

Papa, he also founded West Nottingham Academy in Colora, Maryland, sometime around 1744. Papa says that someday we might take a trip to Princeton," concluded Martha.

"Well, you certainly have interesting ancestors," admitted Carrie, "and it sounds like they were prominent members of society. Do you want me to stand and curtsy?" She laughed gaily.

But Martha was deep in thought. "You know what else, Carrie?" she mused, dipping her fingers in the cool water, and looking solemn. "In Scotland, one of the Finleys was burned at the stake for his Christian faith. Papa and Mama couldn't find out his name, though, even after extended research. Can you imagine being burned at the stake because you love Jesus?" Martha's eyes reflected the horror she felt at her ancestor's fate, and the admiration she had for his willingness to suffer for Christ.

Soon Martha's sister Eleanor came out to the garden to say that Carrie's mother had come to take her home. The girls embraced and said their good-byes to one another. All her guests having left, Martha went inside to help her mother with the washing up.

The following year, the Finley family gained another member—a boy, whom they named Charles. Martha was seventeen years old. In later years, the two were to become very close, in spite of the difference in their ages.

Chapter Four

THE FINLEYS TAKE A TRIP

"MARTHA, HAVE YOU GOT YOUR GREEN SATCHEL?" asked her stepmother. "We'd better hurry! The train is due to leave in ten minutes."

"Yes, Mama. But can you please take Amy's hand for a minute? My bonnet strings have come untied."

"I will tie your bonnet for you, daughter. Hold still a moment," her father said to Martha. "Don't worry, my dear," he cautioned his anxious wife. "We've got a minute to spare. The train won't leave us behind."

As if to belie his words, they heard the voice of the conductor ring out, "All aboard! All aboard!"

Having finished securing Martha's bonnet, Dr. Finley escorted his wife and daughters onto the train and quickly settled them into their seats. Placing their bags, baskets, and satchels in the rack above, he took his own seat just as the train pulled out of the station.

Soon the conductor came through their car, calling, "Tickets! Tickets!" Punching their tickets, he asked if they were comfortable, and receiving their nods and "Yes, thank you's," he moved on, repeating his litany and punching the tickets of newly embarked passengers.

Dr. and Mrs. Finley, Martha, and Amy were taking a trip to visit relatives in Maryland and Pennsylvania. They were traveling on the Baltimore and Ohio Railway, the line that ran from St. Louis to Baltimore. Grandmother Finley, who had come to live with them, had graciously volunteered to stay at home with Charles and Theresa, the two younger children, as Dr. Finley thought the long train trip would be too much for them. The travelers were planning to make a quick stop in Washington, D. C., as none of them had ever visited that city. Neither had any of them traveled by train, so they were all very excited. An accomplished seamstress, Mrs. Finley and her able assistant, Martha, had been sewing for weeks. New pinafores had been made for Amy, and new dresses—trimmed with lace and ruffles—had been stitched together for Martha and her stepmother. Time was even found to make Amy's dolly a new pinafore for the trip. Dr. Finley had shined his boots to a high gloss and pronounced himself ready for whatever the East had to offer.

The Finleys had not seen their Eastern relatives for some time, and were therefore willing to endure the hardships of the steam locomotive—America's newest mode of travel. The wooden seats were straight and hard, and although Mrs. Finley had brought straw cushions to sit on and pillows for their heads, it was still a long and weary trip. Martha, remembering the bumping and jolting of the stagecoach ride she had taken when she was much younger, thought the train a much superior form of travel, hard seats notwithstanding.

The train stopped periodically, but passengers were given only thirty minutes to eat. Mrs. Finley, ever-mindful of her family's needs, had packed a large picnic basket to the brim with fried chicken, corn pone, biscuits, potatoes, and other tasty and nutritious fare to sustain them on the trip. As it was late autumn, and at times quite chilly, the conductor banked a small fire in the wood stove to warm their passenger car.

As they traveled east across Ohio, Martha couldn't contain her excitement. Her readings in history seemed to come to life, as she imagined the life of the early settlers in the areas through which the train was passing. She felt she could almost see the wagons, and the oxen, and the forts, and the Indians. On the other hand, she knew she was living during another great period in her country's history. Wasn't she traveling by train at an unimaginably high speed?

Through the window she enjoyed the beautiful autumn foliage that lined their route for miles and miles. It seemed to her that a great Artist had dabbled his brush in brilliant tones of red, gold, and orange and splashed it over the forests, where it was made all the more striking set against the many shades of green displayed by the evergreens.

Clackity-clack, clackity-clack went the wheels. The seats seemed to get harder and harder with each passing mile. Oh, how she wished for her soft feather bed mattress at home. On the second day of their trip it started to rain, but even through the drops making ribbons down the windowpane, Martha thought she had never seen such beautiful scenery. And so the miles sped by.

Arranging her full skirts about her, Martha spoke softly to her mother, not wanting to disturb her father, who had dozed off. "It will be interesting to see the White House, after having read so much about it. We might even see President Polk," she added hopefully.

"I hope it stops raining," ventured Amy. "We won't be able to see much in the rain."

"I hope the streets of Washington are not rivers of mud. It has rained all day and we have another day of travel yet," sighed Mrs. Finley. Then brightening, she said, "I know something we can do to pass the time! Martha, you're our history student. Why don't you give Amy and I a little history lesson about Washington?"

"I'd be happy to," she said. "Washington was built on land donated by the state of Maryland, and named after George Washington and Christopher Columbus. Who was Christopher Columbus, Amy?"

"The man who discovered America," Amy obediently rattled off in her best schoolgirl voice.

"Very good," responded her sister. "Now, long ago the land Washington is built on was a swamp with only a few scattered villages of the Powhatan Indians . . ." And she continued her narrative until Amy and Mrs. Finley decided they knew just about all there was to know about the city of Washington, D. C. But as Martha always spun a good tale, they were very much entertained and enjoyed hearing what she had to tell them.

The third day they reached the nation's capital. Washington, D. C., turned out to be a disappointment. Mrs. Finley's fears were confirmed—the streets were muddy and there were no walkways. The buildings were bare and stark, and there were few shrubs or trees. Washington, D. C., in the late 1840's, was still a city under construction.

"If only the rain would stop," they kept saying to one another.

They took a coach down Pennsylvania Avenue, past the White House. Martha couldn't take her eyes off it. "Oh, Mama!" she breathed. "I can't believe I'm really seeing the White House! It is so impressive. Oh, how I wish Carrie could be here to see it, too. She and I had a long talk about it once. Oh, Papa, wouldn't it be nice to be able to go inside and see all the grand rooms?"

A twinkle in his eye, Dr. Finley looked at his wife, who responded with a look of amusement. They knew no response was needed. Martha's enthusiasm was carrying the day once again. The ever-questioning child had grown into an endearing young lady whose thirst for knowledge and enthusiasm for the world around her was a marvel to behold. They were also qualities her parents had come to love and appreciate.

Finally, the weather cleared, to the travelers' great relief. They would be able to see the sights of Washington after all. The city was a conglomeration of people. Martha's eyes widened when she saw the rough frontiersman ride by on horseback. She smiled with pleasure when she heard the accent of the lovely Southern ladies, and was delighted to observe the formal manners of the proper New Englanders.

Most of all, Martha and her stepmother enjoyed observing the latest fashions. They admired the colorful sashes, ruffles, and bows, the wide-hooped skirts, the plumed hats, and the exquisite feathered bonnets. One afternoon they were sitting with Amy in the lobby of their hotel waiting for Dr. Finley, who was due back from an appointment, enjoying yet another opportunity to observe the elegant costumes of the hotel's many different guests.

"Oh, Mama, isn't that a beautiful dress?" Martha gestured discreetly in the direction of a guest whose maroon taffeta gown was trimmed with layers and layers of beautifully wrought lace and set off by a sash of deep wine.

"It certainly is, my dear," replied Mrs. Finley. "There must be twenty yards of fabric in it. Some seamstress spent a great deal of time on that dress."

"She must have at least fifty petticoats underneath," added little Amy, thinking how hard it was to manage the few she wore.

"Well, not fifty, Amy, but easily five or six," said her mother with a laugh. "I hope she doesn't have her corset laced too tightly. Sometimes I think fashionable women pay a high price for their elegance. Recently I was reading a magazine article by a doctor, in which he warned us ladies of the dangers of lacing our corsets too tightly. He said it affected circulation as well as digestion and recommended we wear looser clothing. I couldn't agree more."

"Also, Mama, you can't really do much in clothes like that lady is wearing except look beautiful and go to dances," said Martha. "I can't imagine teaching school or helping you with the little ones dressed like that. But it is a beautiful dress, all the same," she concluded.

"Well, my dear, we'll just have to enjoy looking at all the wonderful fashions while we are here. It will give us pleasant memories to carry home and brighten our workdays," said Mrs. Finley with a smile.

Martha's eye was caught by a costume of a different sort. "What sort of outfit is that lady wearing?" she whispered to her mother, indicating a lady strolling through the hotel lobby who was wearing loose-fitting pants under her skirt.

Mrs. Finley, glancing in the direction Martha indicated, smiled again and responded, "Hmmm, those must be bloomers—pants worn under your skirts. I've heard people talking about them, but I've never seen any before. They look pretty funny, don't they? They named them after the woman who first started wearing them—Amelia Bloomer. I wonder if that's who that is!"

Just then, they heard a lady sitting across from them say to her neighbor, "Look! It's Sam Houston—you know, that Texan who captured Santa Anna in the Battle of San Jacinto! He's a United States senator now," she added. As they looked in the direction she was indicating, they saw a tall, distinguished-looking gentleman with greying hair and bright, piercing eyes descending the grand staircase."

Martha's eyes widened. "Sam Houston!" she exclaimed. As she turned back to her mother, she saw another tall, distinguished-looking gentleman coming their way.

Amy recognized him first. "Here's Papa!" she exclaimed. "Now we can have our walk!"

Dr. Finley greeted his family warmly, and gave them a quick account of the visit he had just made. "And I see the three of you have been enjoying your favorite pastime.

"Yes, Papa, and guess what?" Amy looked up at her father, excitement lighting up her face. "We even saw Sam Houston! It sounds like he's somebody really famous, and now he's a sen-a-tor, or something. I think that's what they said," she concluded vaguely. Dr. Finley raised an eyebrow, and then gave a quick wink as if to say, "Well, what do you think of that?"

And off they went on their walk. Although the weather was pleasant, the streets were still muddy from the heavy rain, and in no time at all, the ladies' shoes were a mess, and their skirts were wet and muddy—no matter how carefully they held them up. They agreed to do the rest of their sightseeing by carriage and enjoy a walk when they reached the home of their relatives in Maryland.

On the last day of their sojourn in Washington, as they were on their way to catch the train to Baltimore, they got a peek at President Polk as he rode by in his carriage. Tipping his hat, he waved at them. Martha watched as the carriage rolled out of sight, speechless with excitement. She had actually seen the president of the United States! She could hardly wait to get home and tell young Charles and Theresa about her adventures in the capital city.

The scenes of Washington, D. C., still fresh in their minds, the Finleys boarded a train for Baltimore, where they were to meet some of their relatives. There they had a good visit, met some old friends, and had a restful time. Spending some time in Philadelphia as well, Dr. and Mrs. Finley enjoyed the opportunity of visiting with relatives they had not seen since their marriage. Several times Martha was asked what her plans for the future were, now that her formal education was over. Always she responded by telling the questioner of her great love for children and her plan to become a schoolteacher.

After a thoroughly enjoyable visit, the family started their long train ride home. The doctor mentioned that he did not know when they would ever see their relatives again, as there were so many miles between them. He was very weary by the time they arrived back in South Bend, and Mrs. Finley was worried that the trip had been too much for him. Although he pretended otherwise, he tired easily and lacked some of his former vigor.

Chapter Five

CHILLS AND FEVER

THE MOSQUITOES WERE TERRIBLE. Everyone in town was complaining. Martha and four-year-old Charles were sitting on the front porch swing, trying to stay cool despite the heat of the summer day. Having finished her schooling, twenty-one-year-old Martha was living at home and helping her stepmother with the younger children. Her older siblings had all married and moved away.

Martha was fanning herself and wiping the perspiration from her brow. Wisps of brown curls kept falling in her face. "It is just too hot to breathe today," she sighed.

"It's so hot my shirt is sticking to me," Charles complained. "Martha, would you get me some cold water from the pump? It's too hard for me to pump myself."

"I'll do it in a minute, Charles," said his sister. "It's just too hot to even think about moving from this swing. I don't suppose you have any idea why women must wear long sleeves and high collars in this kind of weather, do you?" She lifted her long skirt slightly to get some air on her legs, wishing she could unfasten her high-buttoned shoes.

"No, Martha," said the little boy, solemnly. "Maybe you need a drink, too."

Martha laughed, and went to fill up two tin mugs with ice cold well water.

When she returned to the porch, she found her little brother holding a jar in his lap. "I caught this big 'skeeter' in my room last night," said young Charles, holding up the jar so she could see the insect inside. "It's a big thing—just look at it! It's about the biggest one I've ever seen!"

"How did it get in? Did it come in through the screen?" asked Martha. "I hope I don't have any in my room." Wiping her brow, she added, "This is the hottest summer I can remember. People say the old swamp is swarming with mosquitoes. I cringe every time I think about them. Put that jar down so I can't see it!"

The Finleys made sure the screens in all the windows fitted tightly and were without holes, as it was too hot to leave the sashes down. Dr. Finley reminded them all to stay far away from the swamp. "If you are bitten by a mosquito," he instructed them, "wash quickly with soap and water and apply a paste of baking soda and water." Although he did not mention this to his family, he was concerned about malaria, a dreaded disease carried by mosquitoes.

One day, he came home certain there was a case of malaria in town. His patient was a young lad of six or seven years who lived not far from the old swamp. "He had a severe onset of the ague," he told his wife. "All his mother and I could do was keep piling blankets on him. Poor little thing."

"What is ague?" asked eight-year-old Amy.

"Severe chills, accompanied by a high fever, headaches, and sweating," responded her father.

"After the attack, there is extreme exhaustion and ane-mia. This little boy's whole body was shaking, and his teeth were chattering so hard he couldn't speak," said Dr. Finley. "I've got to go back later this evening to check on him. I know he has malaria, because I took a blood sample and examined it through my micro-scope." He look tired and worried.

"These people around here keep saying malaria is caused by the night air. Pshaw! That's pure nonsense! Mosquitoes are the carriers. I've said many times that the old swamp should be drained, but no one will lis-ten. I've never seen such an infestation of mosquitoes in all my life!" he said, pacing up and down the room, hands in his pockets. "I'm the only physician in town. If we have an epidemic, I don't know how I'll take care of everyone," he sighed.

"Let's pray to God that it will not happen!" exclaimed his wife.

However, Dr. Finley's fears became reality. Each day that passed found more people stricken with malaria. He went from house to house, administering quinine—the only medicine that helped. Even so, it did not cure the disease, but only suppressed its dreadful symptoms.

"What's quinine?" Charles asked his father one evening, as the family sat in the parlor discussing the deadly illness that was sweeping through the town.

"Quinine is a substance that comes from the bark of the cinchona tree. It's very bitter, and you should pray that you never have to take it. It will certainly make your mouth pucker up," said Dr. Finley to his son, attempting to be lighthearted. Secretly, he was very concerned for his loved ones.

Soon his worst fears were realized. The ague attacked first one, and then another in the Finley family. Everyone came down with the fever, except one of Martha's little sisters and Grandmother Finley. The sick ones all took to their beds. Mrs. Finley nursed her family as much as possible, but some days she was too ill herself. The bitter quinine had to be taken by all. The children balked, but there was nothing to do except take the bitter draught.

Martha, too, succumbed to the disease, and soon grew very weak. She wanted to help her mother, but she simply did not have the strength.

"Martha, you look ready to drop," said Mrs. Finley. "Please lie down before you collapse. You are absolutely white!"

When her father came home, he found Martha drenched in sweat, yet chilled to the bone.

"How are you, daughter?" he asked, trying to keep the worry from his voice.

"Oh, Papa, I feel terrible and I'm so c-c-cold. I w-w-wish I c-c-could help M-m-mama." Her teeth were chattering so hard the words would not come.

Giving her a dose of quinine, he said, "Take heart, daughter. With God's help, everyone will soon be well again."

The ague seemed to strike every other day. Dr. Finley said this was the way it worked. On the day in between, the stricken ones felt better. Neighbors— those who were well—came and went, bringing nourishing food and doing what they could to help. It was said that tomatoes helped get one over the ague. So "tomats," as they were called—cut up, mixed with salt, pepper, and vinegar—were brought, and the family was encouraged to eat.

The housework went undone. There was sand in the carpet, dust on the furniture, and clothing scattered about. Toys were underfoot, chimney globes were unwashed, and a general atmosphere of messiness prevailed. Mrs. Finley was too sick to do much about any of it.

Finally, a girl was hired to come each day to help. She made the beds, dusted, swept, cleaned cobwebs and helped in the kitchen. When trying her hand at the household laundry, however, she failed to separate the colored clothes from the whites, faded the calicoes by her hard rubbing, and ruined the flannels by harsh wringing. Mrs. Finley was aghast and the young helper was sent away crying. Finally an older woman was found, who proved to be completely capable and thorough. Mrs. Finley was now able to stay in bed and get some rest.

The doctor continued to make his rounds among the townsfolk. Finally, utterly exhausted, he was attacked by the dreaded foe and compelled to take to his bed and allow his family to nurse him through the chills, the fever, and the sweats, until he could fall into a weary, deep sleep. Sometimes, even though he was very ill, visitors would come, asking for advice about sick ones at home.

The summer wore on. There was no relief from the heat. It wasn't until early autumn that the world began to look brighter for the people of South Bend, Indiana. Finally, fevers subsided. The Finley family and the other sick townsfolk were at last on the mend. Dr. Finley's strength returned slowly, and it was only gradually that he was able to resume his practice again.

That summer was not soon forgotten. In later years, Martha stated that it remained in her memory as a dreadful dream. It was said that there had never been such a terrible time before and none thereafter.

* * * * *

Months passed. One very cold December afternoon, Martha and her father were sitting by the fire in the parlor. Dr. Finley was reading a newspaper, and Martha was reading Longfellow's *Evangeline*, the poem that had established him as a major American poet upon its appearance two years earlier. Mrs. Finley and young Charles had gone to call on a neighbor and the other two children were in school. Although Dr. Finley's health had improved since his bout with malaria, he was not able to spend long hours at his medical practice, as had formerly been his wont. When the clock on the mantel struck two, Martha looked up from her book. Her father, seeing her pause in her reading, took the opportunity for a little conversation.

"America is expanding, Martha," he said, putting the newspaper in his lap. "The paper says there are thousands of people heading west over the Oregon Trail by covered wagon."

"Yes, Papa, I've read the same thing," Martha replied. "Apparently people are selling everything they have and going west to get free land. I think the trip would be exciting, but very long and tiresome—much longer and much more tiresome than our train trip to the East," she said thoughtfully. "It takes months to get out there."

"Well, I know I'm much too old for that kind of adventure. And I'm quite content to sit right here in my rocking chair," he laughed gently, his eyes twinkling.

"Oh, Papa, you aren't old. I know you haven't been feeling too well lately, but don't give up everything yet," she chided. "But you are right—our country is growing—which is both good and bad," mused Martha, more to herself than to her father. "I read another article in the paper yesterday about missionaries headed west. It reminded me of Dr. and Mrs. Whitman, the missionaries who were killed by Indians a few years ago."

Dr. Finley shook his head. "It's very sad that such a thing happened. The Indians that killed the Whitmans were from a tribe they had been visiting, tending them when they were ill and teaching them about Jesus," he said. He leaned his head back and sighed. Martha thought he looked tired, and made no attempt to continue the conversation. The room felt a little cooler, and she banked the fire. Dr. Finley pulled his shawl a little closer around his shoulders.

Dr. Finley's rocking chair gradually came to a standstill as the tired physician dozed in his chair. Martha continued to sit by his side, her thoughts keeping her company. She couldn't get the Whitmans out of her mind. How terrible, she thought, that the measles had been carried into the territories, and that the Indian children had suffered so much from the disease. A great sigh came from her lips. No medicine had had any effect, and most of the children had died. The Indians thought their children had been poisoned by the very people who had come to help them. "How sad, how very sad," she whispered.

In a while her stepmother returned and together they prepared supper before the girls arrived home from school.

Preparations for Christmas were made. The house was full of the smell of cedar and pine, freshly baked bread and pumpkin pies, smoked ham and roasted goose. The crèche was set up on the mantel, and children and adults alike went about the house humming snatches of their favorite carols. A cold spell continued unabated, but the Finley family celebrated the birth of their Lord with all the reverence and gaiety appropriate to the season.

Some months later, Martha and her mother began their annual spring cleaning. For Mrs. Finley this involved a complete overhaul of the house and its contents, and even the younger girls and four-year-old Charles were assigned tasks. Mattresses were turned, floors and walls were scrubbed, windows were shined, rugs were beaten, and curtains were washed and rehung. Closets and cupboards were cleaned out, linen was washed, bleached, and mended. One morning in the midst of this upheaval, Martha was polishing a table in the parlor and humming a new Stephen Foster tune that had become very popular. The tune was so lively that, without realizing it, she began singing:

"Oh, Susanna, oh don't you cry for me,
I've come from Alabama
With my banjo on my knee.
I come from Alabama
With my banjo on my knee,
I'm goin' to Louisiana
My true love for to see.
It rained all night the day I left,
The weather it was dry.
The sun so hot I froze to death,
Susanna, don't you cry.
Oh, Susanna, oh don't you cry for—"

She was interrupted in mid-song by her younger siblings—busy dusting chair legs and carrying couch cushions outside for a beating—who chorused, "Martha, Martha, teach me the song!" "Yes, teach me 'Oh, Susanna.' " And so the housekeeping was put aside for a singing lesson until Mrs. Finley arrived on the scene and gently steered them back to their unfinished chores.

* * * * * *

The next evening the family was gathered in the parlor, relaxing after yet one more long day of housecleaning. Mrs. Finley and Martha were darning some of the children's socks. Charles, Amy, and Theresa were playing jacks near the windows. Dr. Finley was sitting in the old Boston rocker, its designs of gilt and paint somewhat faded from use. He spent much time with his family now. His eyes were resting on a Currier and Ives print hanging on the wall over the sofa, but his thoughts were in California. They had been discussing the gold rush at dinner, and he was still turning over in his mind some of the things they had been talking about.

The front pages of the newspapers he and Martha read so avidly were full of stories of men that had discovered gold in the far off territory of California. Everyone had "gold rush fever." Towns were springing up overnight—wild, rough towns with wild, rough people. San Francisco had grown from a small village to a thriving city of 25,000 people in only a year's time. Storekeepers were getting rich because people were willing to pay outrageous prices for every imaginable item. Run-down shacks were rented out for $100 a week, and a single cot could cost $15 a night.

"It's outrageous!" exclaimed Martha, picking up the thread of their dinnertime conversation. "Eggs are selling for $1.00 apiece!"

Dr. Finley perked up, eager to return to the topic himself. "It's too much to be believed!" he said. "Some sell absolutely everything they have for a pipe dream and most of them return with utterly nothing. Some will die of disease, or fatigue, or be killed by Indians. Others will freeze in the mountains or die of thirst in the deserts. You know who's getting rich? The storekeepers. The old law of supply and demand says that if you have the goods people need, you can charge whatever price you wish and get it. Thousands of people will lose everything they have, and thousands more never had anything anyway and will come home with only the memory of their great adventure. And a very few will profit from the gold rush by finding gold or selling supplies to the prospectors."

Then, in a lighter tone, he said to Martha, "I heard you singing 'Oh, Susanna' the other day. I hope you're not thinking about taking off for California," he laughed. "I know another one. Want to hear old Papa sing a few lines?" He laughed, then bursting out in a loud but tremulous voice, he sang another popular Gold Rush tune:

"Oh, Sally, dearest Sally!
Oh, Sally, fer your sake,
I'll go to Californy
And try to raise a stake!"

Martha and her stepmother laughed, too. They had-n't heard Dr. Finley sing in years. The younger chil-dren, not certain what their elders found so funny, joined in for the novelty of it. Martha led them all in several other rousing tunes of the day, and then, after prayers, took the children up to bed.

All through 1850 the newspapers wrote of the California gold rush. A few did "strike it rich," but most who went West in search of riches lost everything they had. So many people went to California that by 1850 the territory contained enough people to be admitted to the Union as a state.

Dr. Finley's health continued to decline. He became pale and haggard and, after not too many months, required complete bed rest. Christmas came and went—this one a little quieter than some—and a new year began. Winter turned into spring and the yearly ritual of housecleaning was undertaken once again. This year, great care was taken not to disturb Dr. Finley, who was very weak. His wife and children tend-ed to his every need with cheerful countenances but hearts burdened by the thought of the separation that all knew was not far away.

On May 14, 1851, Martha's beloved father passed away at the age of fifty-seven. He was buried in South Bend, where he had ministered to so many people. Left behind were his wife Mary, Martha, and the three younger children: Amy, who was ten years old, Theresa, who was nine, and Charles, six years of age.

Chapter Six

MARTHA BECOMES A SCHOOL TEACHER

MARTHA WAS TWENTY-THREE years old when her father died. Many changes lay ahead for this well-educated, intelligent, independent thinker. First of all, she needed a job. Upon hearing of a teaching opportunity close to home, she applied and was accepted for the position. Managing a classroom full of children came easily to her—after all, she had been managing her sometimes rambunctious younger siblings most of her life, and she loved children.

A few months later, Mrs. Finley, Martha, and the younger children were enjoying a quiet evening in the parlor. Martha and her mother, sitting in two chairs by the hearth, were trying to make some headway in a huge pile of mending. Amy was reading to the other two children on the sofa across the room.

"Martha," began her stepmother, "we need to talk. As you know, your father left us little more than this house. We can't live on your income as a school-teacher. We need to make some decisions very soon." She paused. "I have given the matter a lot of thought, and I have prayed at length about what should be done. I feel we should return to the East where we will have the assistance of family. I intend to write and inquire what arrangements can be made for us. I have many relatives in the Philadelphia area, and your father's family is there as well." She spoke quietly and tenderly in order not to frighten Charles and the younger girls.

"Of course, Mama, you know I will do whatever is needed," responded Martha.

Her mother gave her a grateful look and picked up her darning needle. "I know you will, my dear. You have been a tremendous blessing to me always, but particularly at this very difficult time." Her eyes were moist as she selected the brown thread with which to darn one of Charles' socks.

"Amy has just finished her story, Mama," said Martha gently. "I think I'll get the children ready for bed and then we can have prayers."

"Thank you, daughter," said Mrs. Finley.

Letters were sent to family members back East, and soon the responses were received, all positive, all welcoming the little family to come "home." Preparations were undertaken. The house and all the furniture was sold, and the rest packed in crates and boxes for shipment back East. The journey East was made by train— Charles and Theresa at last getting their train ride.

It had been decided that Mrs. Finley and the young ones would go to Philadelphia, and Martha would travel to New York to live with her widowed sister Mary and her children. Not wanting to be a burden, Martha secured another teaching position soon after her arrival in New York.

Mary soon decided that something had to be done to give Martha a more "professional" look. Martha had assured her that she did not need any improving, but Mary was not to be deterred. "Let's see," she said one day while they were preparing dinner together, "what can we do with your hair? Why don't you pull it off your face into a neat bun at the nape of your neck? And I'd like to take you to my dressmaker in the city tomorrow so she can fit you for a few fashionable dresses to wear to school next term."

Martha protested. "What is wrong with the dresses I have? They are clean and neat, and they have lots of wear left in them."

"I know, my dear, but teaching in the city is a bit different than it is in a country school. You must get two or three more hats as well, and put away those prairie bonnets," she added. "Yes, we will go to the millinery shop after we leave the dressmaker's."

"But, Mary, I——"

"Now, Martha, no fretting. I will not have my little sister looking like a poor country cousin. The matter is settled."

When Martha's new school year began, she was outfitted with new dresses and new hats. Mary watched approvingly as her "school marm" sister left each morning, delighted that Martha had allowed her to help with her new look.

Martha soon became involved in her sister's church, teaching Sunday school and helping in the church's outreach to the needy. She spent several happy years with her sister and had many pleasant memories of their time together.

It was during this time that Martha began her literary career by writing Sunday school stories and a newspaper article, and it was also during these years that she began to have difficulties with her eyesight.

One day, after Martha had just returned from the oculist, she and her sister were sharing a quiet cup of tea.

"I am so worried about you, Martha," her sister said with some anxiety in her tone. "Whatever are you

going to do? What if you became completely blind—"
She stopped, unable to finish her sentence.

"Well," Martha answered, "with God's help, I would
find a way to cope. I suppose that's where His grace
comes in. In the meantime, I intend to continue to
teach and write and see where that takes me."

"Yes, but do you think you will be able to do that?"
answered her sister. "Didn't the doctor say it would be
quite understandable, considering how poor your eyesight is, if you did nothing at all? What did he call it?"

"Astigmatism. It can be quite a nuisance when I am
reading or trying to write," said Martha. "The letters
get confused, and I have to look away, or close my eyes
for a second, before they go back to their proper position in the sentence. He said I must wear these glasses
all the time, but I know it will take a while for me to get
adjusted to them," she sighed, taking off the spectacles
and rubbing her eyes, as though by so doing she could
make her vision clearer.

* * * * * *

In 1856, Martha journeyed to Philadelphia to visit
her stepmother for awhile, and decided to stay. As the
weeks went by, she devoted more and more of her time
to writing her Sunday school stories. When she gave
some of them to friends and family members to read,
everyone responded with enthusiasm.

"These are good, really good!" said one after
another. "Why don't you see if you can get them into
print. Send them to one of the religious publishers.
It's certainly worth a try," was the litany she heard
again and again.

"They are right," Martha thought to herself. "It's
certainly worth a try." And so she sent in several of her
stories to the Presbyterian Publication Board in
Philadelphia.

Later that year, the Board accepted some of her stories for publication in their Sunday school papers, and soon they began to appear with some regularity. Shortly thereafter, certain magazines began to see the merit of Miss Finley's writing, and her stories reached an ever-widening circle of readers.

In the fall of 1858, Martha accepted a teaching position in Phoenixville, a small town just west of Philadelphia. The new position necessitated yet another move, but this time, although she would have relatives nearby, she would be living independently.

While packing in preparation for her newest adventure, Martha fretted. Packing was not her favorite activity. "Oh my, should I or shouldn't I? Will I need it or won't I? I wish I knew what to take and what to leave behind."

"Martha, who in the world are you talking to?" asked her stepmother, coming into Martha's bedroom. "There's no one here except you. Are you talking to yourself again?" she laughed, giving Martha an affectionate hug. Martha was always glad to have her stepmother's company. Through the years she had proven to be not only a kind and caring mother, but a faithful and loyal friend as well. A decisive and thoroughly practical lady, she was just the one to provide Martha with the assistance she seemed to so sorely need.

"Well, yes I am. You noticed, I am sure," Martha said with a rueful grin, "that I have been answering myself also." Referring humorously to her unmarried state, she continued, "I suppose that really classifies me as an eccentric spinster, doesn't it?"

Not responding to Martha's last remark, Mrs. Finley looked around at the disarray. "What is all the deliberation about, anyway? Are you worried that there won't be enough room for your books?"

"No, Mama," said Martha, putting her arm around her stepmother's waist and leaning her head on her shoulder, "I guess I'm just getting tired of packing and unpacking all the time. I've moved so many times in the last few years. I'm very thankful for the teaching position in Phoenixville, especially as I will be so close to you, but I hope this is the last move for awhile. Each leave-taking is hard, and each settling in to the new place takes some time. It would be a great blessing to be settled in Phoenixville well before the new school year begins."

Turning to a pile of linens on the bed, she began folding some pillowcases.

"I'm sure you will be settled in time, Martha. And perhaps this move will be the last for awhile. Don't be discouraged. God has promised to take care of His children, hasn't He?" Mrs. Finley said, putting her arm around her stepdaughter's shoulder. "He won't let you down, so don't be despondent. Let's just trust God and see what He will do."

"Papa used to say the same thing," Martha said softly. " 'Let's trust God and see what He will do.' Thank you for reminding me of that."

With Mrs. Finley's help, clothes were folded, trunks were filled, and boxes of books and papers were packed and labeled. Martha's bedroom was stripped of all her belongings. She found comfortable lodging in a home near the school, and the move was made.

Martha took great pleasure in setting up her new schoolroom. The room was on the end of the building, and had windows on two sides. On these Martha hung the curtains that her stepmother had given her. At her direction, the janitor placed her small desk in the corner, and arranged the students' desks. Martha placed an inkwell and slate on each desk, and carefully arranged her books on the shelf above her desk. She was ready for the new school year to begin.

The morning of the first day of school found Martha in her long green spring dress with its high neck and long sleeves standing in front of the small mirror in the room that served as her bedroom. She was trying to arrange her hair into a bun at the nape of her neck, and having difficulty doing so, for some reason. "It couldn't be nerves," she thought. "This isn't my first teaching position, after all. But perhaps it is the excitement of another 'first day of school.' " Putting the last hairpin into place, and gently patting the bun to be sure it was secure, she thought back to that day she couldn't get a curl to mind. "Some things never change, I guess," she thought. "I wanted to look my best that day, too."

The walk to the school was a short one from her lodgings, and in less than an hour's time she had met her new students. As the school was private, classes were small. Martha looked at the children and saw seven boys and five girls of varying sizes and shapes, their expressions ranging from timidity and distrust to curiosity and excitement. She wondered which ones would be thirsty for knowledge, and which ones would need to be gently encouraged to work, to try, to fail, to try again, so that success could eventually come.

Gazing at the twelve students that were hers for the year—to teach, to encourage, to love—she smiled and introduced herself.

"Good morning, class. My name is Miss Finley. Welcome to the fifth grade!"

"Good morning, Miss Finley!" chorused the students. Their new teacher was a small lady with wispy hair, a somewhat large nose, and thin lips. Behind the glasses, with their small round frames, were deep eyes that, despite the thick lenses, seemed to peer right into them. They thought she was pretty when she smiled. Later, they never thought about her plainness at all. They simply loved her.

As the year progressed, Miss Finley's students discovered that she had no moods. She was today what she would be tomorrow and what she had been yesterday. Her patience was boundless, they learned, if they were doing their best. If not, they quickly discovered the importance of making a better effort immediately. She never raised her voice, and she never got angry, but every child knew when she was displeased, or worse, when she was disappointed.

Each morning, as her students arrived, Miss Finley would greet them one by one. Looking each one in the eye, she would say, "Good morning, Jim . . . ," "Good morning, Ruthie . . . ," "Good morning, Mary . . ." The students would then take their appointed seats, their teacher would lead them in prayer, and the lessons would begin.

It became a habit at the school in Phoenixville—as it had been in the others at which she had taught—for Martha to tell or read a story to the class each day after lunch. Teacher and students alike looked forward to this time in the school day.

One day, Jim, a tow-headed boy of about ten, said, "Miss Finley, are you going to tell us a story after lunch?"

She smiled—he had forgotten to raise his hand again.

"I like to hear your stories. I bet sometimes you even make them up, don't ya?" he asked, his grin showing a missing front tooth.

A pleasant flush came to her face. "Yes, I do, Jim, but I'll never tell which ones. Would you like me to tell a story right now—before lunch? Let's do it differently today. This one is true and it happened not so very long ago."

Looking around the room she added, "Now, I'd like everyone to get very still. Place your heads on the desks if you wish. This will be a short story, but one with an interesting lesson for all of us."

She paused, gazing fondly at the sea of faces before her. "What a mixture of God's creation is in this class," she mused to herself.

Bringing her thoughts back to the story, she said, "The man's name is George Mueller, and he is still living today. He takes care of orphans. How many of you know what an orphan is?"

Lora, a pretty young girl with pigtails, raised her hand, and Martha indicated that she had permission to answer.

"I think an orphan is a girl or boy who doesn't have anyone to love them, or to tuck them in at night."

"Yes, you're right, Lora, an orphan is a child who has no parents to care for him. George Mueller takes children off the street who do not have parents, and gives them a home in a building that is called an orphanage. Now I am ready to begin my story.

"One morning," she began, "the children had nothing to eat, and Mr. Mueller had nothing to feed them. The plates, cups, and bowls were on the table, but there was nothing to put in them. The children were waiting when Mr. Mueller said, 'Children, you know we must be in time for school.' Lifting his hands toward heaven as he prayed, he said, 'Dear Father, we thank thee for what thou are going to give us to eat this morning.'

"Soon there was a knock at the door. The children's eyes grew wide with anticipation. The door was opened and there stood the town baker with arms full of freshly baked bread. It smelled so good.

" 'Mr. Mueller,' the baker said. 'I couldn't sleep last night and somehow felt you didn't have any bread for the children's breakfast. I got up and baked far into the night. There is plenty for all. Can some of the children help me bring it in off the wagon?' George Mueller looked at the children, smiled, and then thanked the baker for his kindness. The larger boys helped the baker bring in the bread. No sooner had the baker left when there was another knock at the door. One of the children ran to open it. There stood the milkman.

" 'Mr. Mueller,' he exclaimed excitedly. 'My milk cart has a broken wheel. Could you use some milk for the children? I must take all the cans off the wagon and the milk will spoil if it isn't taken inside soon.'

"The children looked at one another. They were seeing God answer prayer before their very eyes. Mr. Mueller thanked the milkman. He then turned to the children and offered a word of thanksgiving to God for their provisions that morning.

"Now, class, that is the end of the story," Martha said. "Someone has given George Mueller the name 'The Man Who Gets Things From God.' Don't you think that is a good name for him?"

"Miss Finley, is that how George Mueller always fed the orphans?" asked Tom, who had listened intently.

Martha replied carefully. "Tom, let's say God fed the orphans. Mr. Mueller was the instrument he used here on earth. Mr. Mueller believed enough to pray and depend on God to do the work."

"That was a lot of children to feed," exclaimed Sally, a little red-headed girl. "Did the children ever go hungry? I mean, was there ever a time when God did not feed them?"

"Not to my knowledge," answered their teacher. "God always takes care of His children one way or another. Does anyone know what Philippians 4:19 says? If you have your Bibles in your desks, let's look up the verses." When the students had found the verse they read it aloud together: "But my God shall supply all your need according to his riches in glory by Christ Jesus." The chorus of young voices reading the beautiful promise of the Scripture brought tears to Martha's eyes.

"Would He do that for us?" asked Tom.

"He certainly would," answered Martha. "Now, let me ask you all a question. If God would do something like that for us, what would He expect us to do?" She looked fondly at the class, waiting for an answer. All the children looked at one another. No one was sure what their teacher meant.

"Well, what did Mr. Mueller do? Did he get upset and worried?"

"No," was Sally's reply.

"Did he fret and complain?"

"No," came the answer from several children.

"What did he do?" inquired their teacher.

Suddenly a hand shot up. "I know, I know!" exclaimed Tom. "I know, Miss Finley. He prayed! Is that right?"

"Hmmm, yes it is, Tom. Good thinking. But—he did something else. Does anyone know? Take a guess," she urged.

The children, perplexed, looked around at one another. Then quietly, and very timidly, a small girl in the back raised her hand.

"Yes, Marjorie?

"Mr. Mueller believed God could do it," Marjorie murmured, lowering her eyes, as if fearful that her answer was incorrect.

Miss Finley smiled with pleasure.

"Exactly right! Very good, Marjorie! George Mueller believed God could do it. That was very good thinking, Marjorie."

Chapter Seven

PEN, INK, AND A KEROSENE LAMP

ANOTHER SUMMER gave way to another autumn. Martha was comfortably established in Phoenixville— teaching school during the week and Sunday school on Sunday. In the evenings, after correcting papers and working on her lesson plans, she wrote out the stories she told to her Sunday school class, stories that she then sent to the Presbyterian Publication Board for their Sunday school papers.

Tonight was no exception. Twilight was fast approaching, and Martha reached over to turn up the kerosene lamp. She had trimmed the wick and cleaned the tall chimney globe that morning, and the soft yellow light shone clearly through the glass.

The flame flickered, and Martha, feeling a slight draft in the room, tucked her long skirts closer about her. The evenings were definitely cooler now. Pushing the corrected papers and her lesson plans to one side, she reached for the pages of the new story she was working on.

Wiping her pen and dipping it into the inkwell, she began to write. The story line was coming together smoothly. She wrote swiftly, with a sure hand. Her imagination fully engaged, she worked far into the evening, oblivious of the time. It grew later, and the room grew cooler. Soon she would need a fire in the fireplace in the evenings for the room to be comfortable, but that was all right with Martha—she loved to work by a cozy fire. Often she longed for more time to write, but her school preparations took much of her time, and she wanted very much to be a good teacher.

Soon she would need to prepare for bed, but there was one thing more she wanted to do tonight. Putting away her story, Martha took up a fresh piece of paper.

"Dear Mary," she wrote to her older sister in New York, "I am well-established, comfortable, busy, and happy. I continue to write. Although I am self-supporting, I find that it is not easy to be a single woman in the late-1850's. Nevertheless, I am very thankful for the education I received—otherwise I might well be doing someone's washing and ironing."

It turned out to be a lengthy letter. Martha inquired about all the family members and asked for all the news. Finally she could no longer keep her eyes open, and closing her letter with blessings and prayers for the safety of her sister and her family, Martha folded her letter and put it into an envelope. Then snuffing out the lamp wicks she prepared for bed. She would have liked to have written more, but she knew she had to be well-rested for the next day's work with her students. And tomorrow there was another letter to answer: her sister Elizabeth in Bedford, Pennsylvania, had written and was eagerly awaiting news of her.

* * * * * *

As her literary efforts became known within the Finley family, a few of the distinguished Finleys became concerned that their relative was pursuing a vocation not appropriate for a lady. Writing, they thought, was strictly a man's career. Soon, Cousin Martha received a visit from one of the more prominent members of her extended family.

It was a cold and dreary afternoon, and it had been a long, tiresome day. The weather had done nothing for the temperaments of her young charges, and on this particular day she had been glad to see them off to their homes. She was longing for a cup of tea, and a few moments to relax.

When her cousin had written asking to call, she had responded promptly, assuring him that he was most welcome and encouraging him to come at his earliest convenience. This was the day that had been decided upon for his visit, and Martha was looking forward to a pleasant time catching up on all the latest family news. Although this particular cousin was not one of her favorites, she felt she would enjoy the companionship and conversation of someone in the family.

As soon as her cousin was announced, however, she felt the atmosphere darken. Ushering him into the parlor, she quietly turned up the lamps, hoping to restore the brightness to the room.

"Won't you have a seat, Cousin Arthur?" she asked. "I am so glad you have come."

"Thank you, Cousin Martha. You are looking well."

"Thank you. I am very comfortable here, and I enjoy my young charges—at least most of the time," she added, thinking ruefully of how out of sorts some of them had been that day. "Would you like some tea?"

"I would, thank you."

Martha excused herself and went into the kitchen for the tea tray. She returned in a moment with the tray, on which she had arranged the tea pot, two pretty china tea cups, and the silver creamer and sugar bowl. Placing the tray on a low table, she served her cousin his tea. After pouring herself a cup, and measuring in the milk and sugar she enjoyed so much, Martha settled back in her chair, ready for a pleasant chat. They talked of this and that, Martha asking him about his wife and children, he asking her about her students, and telling her of the doings of various family members.

Then the tone of the conversation changed.

"My dear Martha," began her cousin in a condescending voice, shifting a little in his seat. "Don't you think your storytelling is getting a bit out of hand?" Reaching a bit for words he wanted, he continued, "It seems somewhat . . . inappropriate. A lady does not do this sort of work." His face wrinkled with distaste. "You must be aware that it won't amount to very much, anyway. We realize you may be trying to supplement your income, but we feel this is not a good way to do it."

"We?" Martha interjected, tilting her head and looking directly into his eyes.

Clearing his throat, straightening his tie, and shifting in his seat again, Cousin Arthur responded. "We in the family, Martha. There has been some discussion. The consensus is that the notoriety of a lady writer in the family could be embarrassing for us. Surely we can work something out," he finished, tightening his lips and giving her a piercing look.

Martha was usually reticent around the more affluent members of the family, whose sensibilities about what was proper and what was not were rather highly developed. Stunned by her cousin's words, for a moment she was completely speechless. Then, sitting a bit straighter and crossing her arms in front of her, her eyes wide with indignation, she responded with some asperity, "I do not feel it is inappropriate, nor is it frivolous. My stories are being accepted and I enjoy writing them. What's wrong with that? I am sorry—I do not want to offend my family—but I do not intend to stop!" Though outwardly poised, inwardly Martha was in turmoil. She could feel her heart beating more rapidly than usual, and knew her pulse was racing.

"Martha, we are concerned about the family name. It is, and has always been, well respected. Many of your ancestors, as you well know, honored God and did much to help our country." He paused for a moment, as if he were trying to consider her point of view. Finally, he spoke again, almost in a pleading tone. "If you can't be persuaded to desist in this endeavor," he said stiffly, "I suggest you consider writing under an assumed name."

To Martha, the room seemed to grow even colder. Wrapping her shawl more closely about her shoulders, she observed her cousin in silence.

Taking a sip of tea, her visitor leaned back in his chair, adding, "Really, Martha, that is the least you can do for the family."

Martha's response was courteous but non-committal. "I will pray about it," she said, and shortly thereafter, the interview was concluded. Polite farewells were exchanged, and Cousin Arthur left. No doubt a report of their conversation would be made to the other "concerned" family members.

As Martha carried the tray containing the tea things to the kitchen, she nearly stumbled. Setting the tray on the counter, she quickly sat down, realizing she was weak with fatigue. Her cousin's visit had been a shock and it had taken every bit of her energy to respond to him calmly. "Here I am, a grown woman of thirty years, shaking like a leaf!" she scolded herself. "Well, at least I told Cousin Arthur what I thought of his consensus. I'm glad I was able to stay calm while he was here! I don't think I could have borne it if I'd given way to tears in his presence." Martha went to bed early that night.

However, as a result of her cousin's visit, Martha began to use a pen name. For the paperback children's books *Lame Letty*, *Learning to Forgive*, and several others, she penned the old family name of Farquharson. Farquharson was the name of her Scotch-Irish ancestral clan, as well as the Gaelic for Finley. Using this name seemed to satisfy her family, and her publisher expressed no objections either.

One evening Martha's friend Sarah, a fellow schoolteacher, came for a visit. Sarah's looks were quite a contrast to Martha's. Her large grey eyes—that seemed to be always smiling—and her full mouth were framed by a cloud of fine hair of the palest gold. She was tall and somewhat angular, though the long full skirts worn by the women of this time did much to soften her angularity. The two women were sitting close to the fireplace, lap blankets across their knees, enjoying a cup of tea and the easy companionship of two friends who have much in common. The drapes had been pulled across the windows, and though the parlor seemed snug, winter's icy drafts still seeped through the protective layers of wood and brick and wool and tapestry cloth.

"Sarah, I wish I had more time to write," Martha confided. "The days are just not long enough. After teaching all day and correcting papers and reviewing lesson plans, there is just not time enough left to write. If I stay up too late, I am tired the next day, and I have less energy for the children. And the other night I fell asleep at my writing desk."

"Would you be able to live on just the money you get from your stories?" asked Sarah. "If so, why not stop teaching and write full time? If you did that, you'd also have more to sell," she pointed out in her practical way, her grey eyes full of reassurance and admiration.

"To be perfectly honest, I don't know what to do," Martha responded. "I enjoy teaching; I love helping children learn. The children are all very special to me. The idea of supporting myself by my writing alone frightens me. Besides, if I wrote all the time, would I have enough to write about? And having poor vision doesn't help any," she added, taking off her glasses and polishing the lenses with a soft white handkerchief.

"Martha Finley, that is the silliest thing I have ever heard you say," proclaimed Sarah. "Why, stories just seem to flow out of you. In case you've forgotten, our nation is in a state of terrible unrest. There's talk of a civil war. If that happens, our country will be torn apart! You'll have plenty to write about. Families will be torn apart, brothers will fight brothers, sweethearts will become estranged. Write about that, and the terrible hardships such a war would cause." She added, with some vehemence, "Put on your thinking cap!"

Martha was encouraged by her friend's confidence in her ability to write. Replacing her glasses, she replied, "Yes, I know you're right. Perhaps I've not enough confidence of my own. Thank you for having some for me. I really should give this whole matter a good amount of prayer."

* * * * * * *

The winds of a civil war were gathering force. Everyone was talking about what would happen if war came. The school officials called a meeting of teachers and parents.

Standing before the group, the headmaster made an alarming announcement. With some hesitation, and no little emotion, he said, "Due to the perilous state of affairs in our country, with the strong possibility of armed conflict breaking out at any time, we feel it would be wise to close the school at the end of this term until further notice. We sincerely regret this action, for the sake of students and teachers alike, but we feel we have no other choice."

The parents and teachers were stunned by the announcement, having had no intimation that closing the school was even being contemplated. A heated discussion ensued, many saying that such action should not be taken on simply rumors of a war, others insisting that the difficulties would never result in open conflict, but would be resolved peaceably. But the decision of the school officials was not affected by the pleas of the parents, and the school was closed at the end of the term.

So again, after having been in Phoenixville for some two years, Martha found herself unemployed. She moved back to Philadelphia and her stepmother. Choosing not to seek another teaching position, she decided to devote herself to her writing. It was not an easy decision. Although she had had some success as a writer and people such as her friend Sarah believed in her and encouraged her, there was a certain social stigma against women writers at the time. Even though her cousin Arthur lacked grace and compassion, social convention was on his side.

From this time on her pen never stopped. She continued writing her Sunday school stories, among which were "By Their Fruits Ye Shall Know Them," "Little Dick Positive," and "Stupid Sally, the Poor House Girl." She also wrote several novels that, sadly, never received much attention in the literary world.

One day Martha called on her publisher. Entering the offices, she was accosted by the cashier, who said, "Miss Martha Farquharson, I believe?"

"Yes, sir," Martha replied.

"I believe we have a check for you," he said, and turning, went into a back room. He returned with a puzzled expression on his face. "No, I am mistaken. The check is made out to a Miss Finley."

Martha laughed and explained that although Miss Farquharson wrote the stories, Miss Finley accepted the checks given in payment for them. Then, seeing the confusion in the cashier's eyes, she relented, and explained that Miss Finley and Miss Farquharson were one and the same.

* * * * * * *

In 1861, the year Martha celebrated her thirty-third birthday, and after many months—actually years—of tension between the Northern and the Southern states, civil war broke out. Abraham Lincoln had been elected the fall before, and for many in the South, his election tipped the scales in favor of secession. It has been said that the primary cause of the war was the issue of slavery. Although some say that if slavery had not been an issue there would have been no war, in reality there were a number of reasons that arms were taken up. The South believed the Constitution gave her the right to withdraw from the Union, and Lincoln was determined that the Union should be preserved. Congress did not declare war on the Confederate States of America; rather, Abraham Lincoln called for troops from the Northern states. Few people—in the North or the South—thought the war would go on for four long and bloody years, that so many lives would be lost, and that the South would at the end of it all lie in ruins.

But in that summer of 1861, those grim realities were yet to come. The air was warm and fragrant with flowers, birds were calling one to another, and everywhere trees and shrubs were spreading forth their leaves and lush foliage.

One afternoon Martha received a visit from her friend Sarah, who had moved back to the city also. Martha was grateful for Sarah's steady friendship, and always looked forward to her visits. Removing her hat and light shawl, Sarah allowed her petite friend to show her into the front parlor and settle her into a comfortable seat that faced the wide, front windows that were open to the summer breezes. The room was a comfortable one. The soft tones of the woodwork and walls blended unobtrusively with the pattern of the large rug, the Currier and Ives prints—one of the few treasures Mrs. Finley had been unwilling to sell before she left South Bend—added depth and interest to the room, and the generously upholstered furniture promised relaxing and enjoyable conversation.

"I'll just be a minute," Martha promised. "I have a treat for us!" She left the room and returned shortly with two cool glasses of lemonade and a plate of fresh cookies.

"Oh, how special, Martha! Thank you!" exclaimed Sarah. Sarah was very fond of cookies, and somehow they never did a thing to make her less angular, much to Martha's dismay, because they did a great deal to make her even rounder than she was. But she put that unwelcome fact out of her mind and helped herself to a cookie after she had offered them to Sarah.

"How's your writing these days?" Sarah asked her friend, as soon as they were comfortably settled for a chat. "Are you still burning the midnight oil?" she teased.

Martha retorted with a laugh, "Yes, I am. And how is your teaching? Did you enjoy your year at the new school?"

"I did, and the teaching went very well. My little charges were as lively as ever, and I'm looking forward to the fall."

Their talk turned on those things of interest to them both. As they returned to the subject of Martha's writing, Martha was generous in her acknowledgment of Sarah's role in her career as a writer, saying,

"You were right, Sarah. I have more ideas to write about than I dreamed possible, now that this war has started. I can write about President Lincoln—what he says, what he does, where he goes. I could also write about his wife, Mary Todd Lincoln. There always seems to be an article in the newspaper about her. They say she wears the grandest gowns. Women will always be interested in fashion, regardless what else is going on."

Returning to the topic of the war, she continued, "This terrible war makes me both sad and angry. It's just not right for us to fight each other, and it is absolutely horrid for one person to own another. God created us all equal. I know I could write something on that subject!" she exclaimed, her cheeks flushed with determination. "But, on the other hand, how would I fit that into children's stories?" Then, smiling playfully, she asked, "Have you read that Mr. Lincoln has grown a beard? It's all over the newspapers."

Sarah laughed. "Yes, I have. I read that a young girl from New York wrote Mr. Lincoln a letter telling him he'd look better if he grew whiskers. Let's see, what was her name?"

"Grace Bedell, I believe," responded Martha, as she reached for another cookie.

"That's right, I remember now. Well," Sarah continued, "I think it's rather amazing that a young girl could be the reason a president would decide to grow a beard. And she told him she would try to persuade her brothers, who are Democrats, to vote for him. It reminds me of the Scripture 'a little child shall lead them.' Frankly, though, I think he does look much better with a beard."

The two women talked long into the afternoon, two friends able to speak unreservedly to one another, sharing their thoughts and offering one another encouragement. They discussed what they could do to help in the war. The Northern states were fighting against their Southern neighbors. Sarah stated bluntly that she was not moving out of the free state of Pennsylvania because she agreed with President Lincoln.

Changing the subject a little, Martha asked, "Have you seen the green paper money the bank is giving out instead of coins? Using paper money will be difficult to get used to, don't you think?"

"I agree," said Sarah. "The government is calling them 'greenbacks.' Apparently they will be used to help with expenses for the war. Let's see, I was reading something about that the other day. People are saying that these greenbacks cannot be exchanged for gold, or silver either. Makes me wonder if they are going to have any value at all." She chuckled. "Let's just see what happens when we try to use them down at the general store. You know, old Mr. Haines hasn't changed a thing in a hundred years."

Rolling her eyes, Martha remarked quite seriously, "Well, I can understand a little of how he feels. Sometimes all these new ideas scare me. People are saying that one day a man will actually fly around in the sky, just like the birds. Can you imagine that?"

Sarah had turned her attention to the front page of a newspaper lying on the floor beside her. Martha had been reading it earlier in the day and had not yet put it away. "Well, look at this!" she exclaimed, pointing to a newspaper article. "They've strung telegraph wires all the way to California!"

"What's a telegraph?" asked Martha.

"It's a machine invented by a man named Samuel Morse that sends messages to people far away. At first they couldn't send them so far, but now I guess they can go all the way across the country. I don't understand how that can be done. And here's something else. According to this article, inventors are working on a machine that will carry voices over distances.

"When they get it perfected, people will be able to talk to each other from one end of town to the other. I just can't comprehend all this!" exclaimed Sarah, her forehead wrinkled in consternation.

"There go the smoke signals and the Pony Express," Martha laughed. "We certainly won't need them anymore. They'll be antiques! Remember last year when they were advertising for Pony Express riders? I think the ad went something like: 'WANTED: Young, skinny, wiry fellows. Not over 18. Must be expert riders, willing to risk death daily. Orphans preferred. Wages: $25 per week!' That was certainly good pay, but the job was really dangerous."

Growing more serious, she added, "I suppose the telegraph could help in the war effort, though."

"In what way?" inquired Sarah.

"The government needs good communication. California is a state now, you know, and though it is far away, President Lincoln will need to be in contact with the state government. It seems to me, the telegraph would be the fastest way to do that," Martha replied.

After a moment of companionable silence, Sarah asked Martha, "What is the cause of this war anyway? Is it really being fought over the issue of slavery? Some people are blaming it all on Harriet Beecher Stowe and her novel *Uncle Tom's Cabin*. President Lincoln, when he met Mrs. Stowe, even said, 'So you're the little woman who wrote the book that made this great war.' I'm sure he was joking, but still, it makes you wonder."

"According to what I have read, slavery is one of the big issues, but it is not the only one. One of the biggest issues is economic. There's a great rivalry between our industrial Northern states with their factories and our agrarian Southern states with their plantations. Each of the sections has a very different way of life, and there has been a struggle for dominance, especially in Congress. One article said that right now our United States is composed of eighteen free states and fifteen slave states. Every time a new state comes into the Union, the balance of power is threatened. The tension has been building for years and now it has come to a head. I am really afraid for our country," Martha added despairingly. "The Southern states believe they have a constitutional right to secede, and apparently they're willing to fight to defend that right. Since the Northern states have threatened to secede on more than one occasion, there must be something to that. It's just so complicated. President Lincoln calls the country 'a house divided . . . half slave and half free,' and that is true. And I think every man, no matter what color, should be free. But the thought of war is horrifying to me."

"I agree," responded Sarah, "but I believe we must take a stand. Remember that Mr. Lincoln said, 'Stand with anybody that stands right. Stand with him while he is right and part with him when he goes wrong.' "

"Only a school teacher would remember that, Sarah," said Martha with a laugh. Hoping to lighten the mood, she continued, "I do say I must give you an A-plus for your recitation! And now, my dear, I think it's time for tea! The evening is well upon us."

* * * * * * *

The War between the States dragged on for four long years—from 1861 to 1865. Martha continued to write, often late into the evenings. She kept abreast of the terrible events of the times by faithfully reading the newspapers and as many magazines as she could find.

One Sunday in church she heard a hymn that was new to her. When she asked the choir director about it, he told her that it had been written by the famous Julia Ward Howe. Sometime later she read an article in the *Atlantic Monthly* about Mrs. Howe and discovered that this well-known writer and social reformer had written

"The Battle Hymn of the Republic"—as the hymn was called—after visiting military camps near Washington, D.C. As she heard it on subsequent occasions, she became familiar with it, and her stepmother often found her softly singing the lyrics:

Mine eyes have seen the glory of the coming of
    the Lord;
He is trampling out the vintage where the grapes
    of wrath are stored;
He hath loosed the fateful lightning of His terri-
    ble swift sword;
His truth is marching on.
Glory! Glory! Hallelujah! Glory! Glory!
    Hallelujah!
Glory! Glory! Hallelujah! His truth is marching on!

Truly the song was on the lips of many of the Northern soldiers and people who favored the Union cause. The Southerners preferred "Maryland, My Maryland." The music of the times was one more manifestation of the great chasm that had opened between the North and the South.

One day in the spring of 1865 Martha was returning home after a walk. As she turned into her front walk, she saw a young boy running up the street, shouting, "It's over! It's over! The war's over! My father's coming home!" Like the town crier he was for the moment, he continued, "General Lee has surrendered to General Grant in Virginia. Hooray! The war's over!"

The war was indeed over. The North had preserved the Union, but the South was in ruins—its land was completely destroyed. Desolation was everywhere: the policy of "total war" pursued by the North left plundered homes, grieving women, wives and mothers of men that would not return, homesteads burned to the ground, horses and livestock killed or stolen, trampled gardens, ruined fields. The economy was shattered and the means for rebuilding it were nonexistent. The state of Mississippi alone spent one-fifth of its revenue on artificial arms and legs for its returning wounded soldiers. People made clothing from their curtains, and printed newspapers on the back of wallpaper. Southern resources were nonexistent, and inflation soared. Shoes cost as much as $200 per pair, and a barrel of flour skyrocketed to $300. Little of the fighting had occurred in the North, and it had not been subject to a blockade, so it fared much better. Its losses, while great in terms of human life, materially were negligible.

The surrender of the South, on April 9, 1865, was one of the most dramatic moments in American history. On that day, Robert E. Lee, the great Southern general, officially surrendered to Ulysses S. Grant in a farmhouse in Appomattox Court House, Virginia. General Lee had dressed carefully, wanting to appear at his best, thinking he would be taken prisoner. He held his head high, knowing he had fought his best. Strapped to his side was a beautiful shining sword, which, according to the rules of war, the defeated general was to relinquish to the winner.

The official terms of surrender were written out. General Grant was very generous. He did not take the sword of his opponent, and he allowed General Lee to go free. The Southern soldiers surrendered their weapons, but were allowed to keep their horses, at General Lee's request. After being given a full day's rations, they started the long trek homeward.

* * * * *

Five days later, Martha was sitting at her writing desk. It was cool for April, and a small fire was burning in the fireplace. There was a knock at the door.

Laying aside her pen, she rose to open it. On the porch stood the young son of the family across the street. His expression was sober.

"Yes, Frank, what can I do for you?"

"Sorry to bother you, Miss Finley," he said. "My mother wondered whether you'd heard the news. She asked me to come over and tell you." He seemed to be having some difficulty delivering his message, and finally gulped out, "President Lincoln was shot last night."

"What?" gasped Martha. "Our president was shot? Is he dead? How? Who would do such a thing? Why?" she exclaimed as she put her hands to her face.

"I don't know, Miss Finley. I only know he was shot. The president is dead."

"How in the world did it happen?"

"Well ma'am, the president was attending Ford's Theater in Washington. The man just sneaked up from behind and shot him in the head." With anguish in his face, he continued, "They say Mrs. Lincoln is in a terrible state."

With a thread of fear in her voice, Martha spoke, "Oh dear, what is happening in our country? Oh dear!"

Reading a few days later about the details of President Lincoln's last hours, Martha was touched deeply by Mr. Lincoln's last words to his wife. The paper reported that Lincoln told her that "he wanted to visit the Holy Land and those places hallowed by the footprints of the Saviour. He was saying there was no city he so much desired to see as Jerusalem." Martha read on, unconsciously saying the words aloud: "And with the words half spoken on his tongue, the assassin's bullet entered the brain, and the soul of the great and good president was carried by the angels to the new Jerusalem above."

Tears flowed down her cheeks as she whispered, "Dear God, this is the time when we needed him most.

We needed him to reunite our country and heal the scars of war. What a terrible thing has been done."

Chapter Eight

A Girl Called Elsie Dinsmore

Abraham Lincoln had drafted the "Gettysburg Address."

Louisa Mae Alcott was penning *Little Women*.

Harriet Beecher Stowe was still enjoying the phenomenal success of *Uncle Tom's Cabin*.

Martha Finley was creating the unforgettable *Elsie Dinsmore*.

Martha had been writing for nearly fourteen years. Her stories, printed in Sunday school papers and newspapers, were gaining in popularity.

Today she was lying in bed. She had taken a bad fall and had injured her back. Her doctor had ordered complete bed rest, which necessitated absolute dependence on her sister Eleanor's family, with whom she was now staying. Eleanor had been fussing over her all morning.

Martha said to her, as she came into the room yet another time, "I am so sorry to be such a nuisance. It seems all my life others have had to worry about me. Please don't bother yourself so much. I will really be all right."

Eleanor, setting a pitcher of cold water on the night stand, chided her. "Little sister, you are no bother. Please accept my help until you are on your feet again. See what a lovely day it has turned out to be? Just lie quietly and enjoy the scenery through the window. Look—there is a blue jay on the branch of that tree! Can you see it?"

"Yes, Eleanor, I can. And thank you for reminding me to count my blessings. I think I will sleep awhile now."

Eleanor gently adjusted the bedclothes and quietly left the room.

But Martha was worried, although she told no one. While convalescing, she prayed for God's wisdom in writing a book that would sell well enough to enable her to support herself completely.

After much prayer, a new idea came. She would write a story about a young heiress who lived on a Southern plantation. The heroine would be pretty, sweet, and lonely, blamed for her mother's death and deserted by her father. One afternoon, she quickly jotted down notes and was thankful that she was skillful at sketching characters and developing plots.

Elsie, as she named her young heiress, was modeled after two nieces. One had a lovely temperament and the other a lovely face, big beautiful eyes and lovely brown curly hair. She blended the two and created Elsie Dinsmore: a young heroine with an exceptional Christian character. For over three years Martha prayed and worked on her story, saying little about it, and continuing to submit her other stories to her publishers.

* * * * * * *

"So you've finished," said Charles by way of a greeting, as he walked into the room. Martha was sitting at her desk, going over some last-minute adjustments to her manuscript. "I must say, dear sister, you have worked hard on this one," he continued with a grin. "May I read some of it?"

"Not yet," she responded. "I don't know whether I'm ready to have it read by anyone. I think it isn't quite good enough. I think it needs more polishing."

Laughing, Charles said, "Martha, that's what every author says. Authors are never quite finished—there is always something to change or add. But I suppose I will just have to be content to wait for the finished product."

Martha was appreciative of Charles' interest. Though he had now, at twenty-two years of age, grown into a handsome young man who had many demands on his time, he still took the time to visit his older sister and encourage her in her literary efforts.

"I suppose I am just afraid of a rejection slip on this one. There have been a few, you know," said Martha wistfully.

"Martha, you have sold many, many stories. Your name is known in the literary world. This may be that 'open door' you have been praying for. Just trust God and see what happens. You must have faith in yourself, and in God," he remonstrated.

"I know, Charles. Thank you for your encouragement. You are a great help to me."

Charles continued, "I know God has given you the gift of writing. You have been willing to work hard to develop it. Now you must move in the spirit of faith and 'Trust God and see what He will do.'"

Martha was very appreciative that she and Charles were so close. The seventeen years' difference didn't seem to matter to either one of them.

* * * * *

In 1867 the "Elsie Dinsmore" manuscript was submitted to Dodd, Mead Publishers, in New York. Martha was thirty-nine years old, and still living in the Philadelphia area.

Months went by. Finally, one morning the mail brought a reply from the publisher. Margaret, one of Eleanor's daughters, entered the front hall and found her aunt sorting through the day's mail.

"Oh, Auntie, is there a letter for me?" she asked plaintively.

"Well, let me see. There just might be one for you here. Were you expecting something from anyone in particular?" she asked mischievously, knowing that Margaret had a beau who was away on business. Suddenly Martha's eye caught sight of a letter postmarked New York. For a moment she stood very still. Her heart fluttered and her eyes widened.

Seeing the return address, Margaret exclaimed, "Open it, Auntie, open it!"

With fear and trembling, Martha quickly opened the letter and read its contents.

"They accepted it! They accepted it! Margaret, can you believe it?" Martha held the letter to her bosom. "It says they have discussed my book with their editors, and want to publish it in the near future, with the readership directed toward young girls. Editing will begin immediately, and I will be hearing from them soon concerning other suggestions, and the legal aspects of publication."

Martha and Margaret were crying, tears streaming down their cheeks, and embracing each other for sheer joy. How good God was!

"Auntie, how wonderful for you!" exclaimed Margaret. "What a blessing, after all your hard work. Praise the Lord for His goodness. The Bible does say that God will give us the desires of our hearts if we trust Him. I am so happy for you."

A few weeks later a second letter arrived, dealing with business matters related to the publishing venture, and containing also an unexpected note. The publisher intended to divide the huge manuscript into two books. The suggested title for the second was, *Elsie's Holidays at Roselands*. It was to be released one year after the first.

One day Martha said to Eleanor, "I am going to New York next week."

"Whatever for?" asked her sister. "Martha Finley, sometimes you get the strangest notions."

"I know," said Martha with a laugh, "but I've been thinking about this for more than a week. I have a request to make of my publisher. I know it's crazy, but I'm going to try," she said with determination.

"What is your request?" Eleanor asked.

"Well," said Martha, "I'd like the covers of my books to have pansies on them."

"What on earth for?" exclaimed Eleanor. "I mean, why pansies? And anyway, you have no business going to New York alone!"

But Martha was not to be deterred. She had made her decision, and no objection from Eleanor was going to change her mind.

At the end of the week, dressing carefully in her brown and green traveling suit and its matching hat, she took a carriage to the train station. The trip from Philadelphia to New York took only a few hours. It was a determined, but weary Martha Finley who finally took her seat in her editor's office at Dodd, Mead.

"Tell me now, Miss Finley," said Mr. Maxwell, after they had exchanged pleasantries and Martha had made her request. "Why are you suggesting that your Elsie Dinsmore books have some type of 'pansies' on the cover?" Clearing his throat, he continued, "You did say pansies, didn't you? Why pansies, and not roses, for instance?"

Sitting a bit taller in her chair, smoothing her long skirts and holding her purse tightly, Martha said firmly, "I just like the idea. Pansies mean 'thoughts of you.' Certainly I have put much thought into this book."

Rubbing his ear and leaning back in his chair, Mr. Maxwell replied, "Hmmm, a strange request indeed. I've never had one like this before. However, we shall see." Then with a faint smile he added, "Even stranger, Miss Finley, that you traveled this distance just to discuss it with me." He paused. "You do understand that I cannot promise anything. We have made the decision to print the book covers in both blue and red. I suppose some sort of pansy could be printed on them, and at an added expense." Then leaning forward quickly, he added, with doubt shadowing his voice, "But of course, as I have said, I cannot promise anything."

Martha sighed with relief when the interview was over. It had taken much courage for her to go, but on the train ride home she more than once reviewed her chat with the editor at Dodd and Mead. Finally—her old independent spirit rising up—she said to herself, "I tried, and that editor doesn't know everything. I shall make this a matter of prayer. It may be a small thing, but God has been good, and I will trust Him again. Mama always says, 'Prayer changes things.' "

One morning, many months later, the postman brought a large package with a New York postmark. "Good morning Miss Finley," the carrier said courteously. "You have a package today. Would you sign here please?" Waiting hesitantly on the threshold, he added, "Folks around here don't often get packages. Have any idea what it is?"

Martha knew exactly what it was, but decided this was going to be her little secret for a while longer. Thanking him courteously, but without responding to his question, she closed the door and hurried into the parlor.

Quickly tearing away the brown wrapping, she opened the box, her eyes wide with anticipation. There they were! Elsie Dinsmore—copies in red and blue, one of each. Her countenance fell, for at first glance there were no pansies. But looking closer, she saw them, in vague embossing: pansies, all over the covers!

"Oh thank you, Lord," she whispered. "You have answered even the simplest of my prayers." Carefully and tenderly she examined her treasures. Then she bowed her head and let the tears fall.

Chapter Nine

BEYOND HER WILDEST DREAMS

OVERNIGHT SUCCESS! That's what the newspapers were saying. *Elsie Dinsmore* was sweeping the country. Every young girl wanted to read it and the mothers wanted it too—Elsie was a good role model for their daughters. Neither Martha nor her publishers were ready for the sudden popularity of the book.

Elsie's Holidays at Roselands, the sequel to *Elsie Dinsmore*, was published the following year. In 1868, the publisher proclaimed *Elsie Dinsmore* their best seller. Martha Finley, its author, was now forty years old.

Many family members gave encouragement and support, and expressed their congratulations. Her stepmother and all her siblings were very proud and happy for her. Those who could not express their happiness in person sent congratulatory notes and expressions of love. Some family members, however, still proclaimed that writing 'frivolous stories' should not be done by a lady of Martha's social standing.

But Martha did not rest on her laurels for a moment. She was already writing a third book in what was to be known as the Elsie series. Her pen was never idle. From time to time she would have to stop, lay her pen aside, and give her eyes a rest. When her vision cleared she would again take up her pen and continue the saga of the beloved Elsie.

The Elsie books were to bring much change into Martha's life. For some years, she had been living in genteel poverty, as her previously published works had not brought in sufficient income for her to live alone. This was no longer to be the case.

* * * * * * *

The world was expanding. The War Between the States had been over for three years. Both the North and South were rebuilding, in spite of bitter feelings on both sides. Abraham Lincoln had been dead for three years. The life of the common man was hard. He started work early and finished late. There were few conveniences. One could not yet switch on an electric light: it would be fourteen years before Thomas Edison invented the light bulb. The radio was also an invention of the future. Horse and buggy was still the main mode of travel. The first car would not be invented until twenty-two years later. Even the bicycle as we know it today was not yet seen on the city streets.

There was no television for Martha to watch and no telephone for her to use—although there was discussion of some kind of "talking machine." The first flight of the Wright Brothers was thirty-six years away. And there was no typewriter. Martha had written all these years with pen and ink.

* * * * * *

Real popularity came in 1869, when Elsie Dinsmore became a household word. Everyone was reading about the poor little rich girl.

"Why do you think my adult novels are not selling?" Martha asked her stepmother, who was visiting. "I have written a number of them, and none seem to be appealing to the public. I really thought people would like *Casella*. I would so like for people to know about the persecution of believers so many years ago."

"I don't understand it either, Martha. I remember you speaking of the amount of research and labor that went into *Casella*. Weren't the reviews flattering?" Mrs. Finley asked soothingly.

"Yes, but the sales weren't. *The Blue Morocco Shoes* was a good story too, and so was *Hugo and Franz*. I just don't understand why people don't buy them. I suppose I had better just write for children, as that's where my success lies. Evidently, people didn't enjoy my historical novels," she mused.

"I do have another idea," Martha continued. "I have long desired to write about the problems of boys as well as girls. I would like to write of the struggles of a typical boy about Elsie Dinsmore's age. What do you think?" she asked her stepmother.

Mrs. Finley encouraged her daughter, and as always, offered helpful comments and wise counsel. The result was *Old-Fashioned Boy*, a book about a well-mannered boy named Fred, who suddenly finds himself called upon to take responsibility for his mother and sister after the death of his father. His mother's subsequent remarriage to a selfish man who misuses Fred's inheritance causes him great concern, but through it all, he is an example of obedience, self-restraint, and loyalty. This book, too, was successful, and the publishers soon asked for a sequel, which Martha had not originally had any intention of writing. The second book she called *Our Fred*.

Another novel, *Wanted: A Pedigree*, was published in 1871. Martha had great hopes of its success, but it received very little attention.

In 1872 *Elsie's Girlhood*—the third Elsie book—was published. Martha was now forty-four years old—and famous. In the preface of *Elsie's Girlhood*, she wrote,

> May my readers who have admired and loved her as a child find her still more charming in her fresh young girlhood; may she prove to all a pleasant companion and friend; and to those of them now treading the same portion of life's pathway a useful example also, particularly in her filial love and obedience. (1872)

In the winter of 1873-74, Martha laid down her pen to take a well-deserved vacation. Feeling she needed to get away, she decided to visit her sister Elizabeth, who lived in Bedford, in the western part of Pennsylvania.

Elizabeth had written in a letter to Martha how much she was looking forward to her visit, how greatly she was anticipating sitting by the warm fire and enjoying good conversation with her. Realizing that winters in Philadelphia were not as severe as those in her area, she had said in her letter, "Pack your warmest clothes—long, warm stockings, and your strongest, warmest shoes. Bring your woolen dresses and shawls. The winter winds send chills to the bone, and this old house has many chilly drafts. By all means wear your heaviest, warmest coat and gloves on the train. I do not want my little sister to arrive with frostbite and a red nose!"

The day after Martha's departure, one of Pennsylvania's worst blizzards in years began. Looking at all the large drifts from the train window, Martha was glad she was safe and warm inside. At the same time, she could hardly wait to reach her destination.

Thankfully she arrived in Bedford before the worst had hit, so the rails were still open. The drifts were high, however, and the blasts of wind almost knocked the tiny lady off her feet. Once inside her sister's farmhouse, she did not venture out for a week. Elizabeth's children came to visit their famous aunt, however; they were used to traveling in the snow. Martha and Elizabeth spoke of their brother Samuel and wondered how he was, as no one had heard from him in a long while. They laughed over their childhood memories of Samuel and his trials in growing up with four sisters. Martha stayed in Bedford for the winter months, visiting back and forth between Elizabeth and an aunt who also lived in the vicinity. After a refreshing rest, she returned to Philadelphia and her writing.

* * * * *

Spring arrived, then early summer. Martha and her sixty-seven-year-old stepmother were sitting on the porch swing, sipping lemonade.

"Do you realize you are a famous woman, Martha?" asked Mrs. Finley. "Not even to mention the money you are making."

"Yes, I suppose that is true, Mama. I still pinch myself to see if this is really happening to me. I can't believe that the readers still want more Elsie adventures. The newspapers say that *Elsie Dinsmore* is one of the most popular books ever written," she said in a thoughtful tone as she sipped her lemonade.

"Are you going to make it a series?" asked Mrs. Finley with a mischievous grin.

"I intend to keep on as long as my young readers want more. I have all kinds of adventures for Elsie in mind. My theme has been love and Christian faith, but I have put in some romance—such as engagements and weddings—to make the story more interesting. Young girls like that," Martha concluded.

"Well, my dear, you seem to have a great influence on public opinion," smiled her stepmother.

"Mama, I just want to make real for girls that God is their Father and Protector. I suppose too, that Elsie Dinsmore is a child's struggle for right in a not-so-right world," said Martha. "I hope to provide my young readers with a compassionate friend. And the money I make will help me repay you for all your kindness and support over the years. I haven't forgotten that."

The public and the publishers were asking for more. The fourth book—*Elsie's Womanhood*—was published three years later, in 1875. In the preface, Martha explained why she had written yet another book about Elsie Dinsmore:

> The call for a sequel to *Elsie's Girlhood* having become too loud and importunate to be resisted, the pleasant task of writing it was undertaken.

Commenting on her inclusion in the book of the Civil War, and the bitter feelings that caused it and that remained afterwards as a result of it, Martha told her readers:

> Dates compelled the bringing in of the late war: and it has been the earnest desire and effort of the author to so treat the subject as to wound the feelings of none; to be as impartial as if writing history; and by drawing a true, though alas, but faint picture, of the great losses and sufferings on both sides, to make the very thought of a renewal of the awful strife utterly abhorrent to every lover of humanity, and especially of this, our own dear native land.

Are we not one people: speaking the same language; worshipping the one true and living God; having a common history, a common ancestry; and united by the tenderest ties of blood? And is not this great, grand, glorious old Union—known and respected all over the world—our common country, our joy and pride? O! let us forget all bitterness, and live henceforth in love, harmony and mutual helpfulness. (1875)

* * * * *

Charles and Martha were discussing *Elsie's Womanhood*. He had moved to Elkton, Maryland, where he lived with his wife, Rebecca. Today he had come by train to the city on business, and as was his wont, he had stopped to see Martha while in town. Upon his arrival, he found his sister sitting in her usual place—pen in hand. Putting aside her writing, she welcomed him with a hug, then settled down in her favorite chair, ready for a comfortable chat with her brother.

"Did you enjoy *Elsie's Womanhood,* Charles?" she asked him.

"I did, indeed, Martha, and Rebecca did also," he replied. Continuing, he commented, "And I appreciated the preface very much. I agree with what you said about forgetting 'all bitterness,' and hope that what you write has some good effect."

"I do too, Charles. Because so many people read my books, I feel I should take the opportunity to do what I can to encourage harmony."

"I can think of no place that stands more in need of healing than Maryland. You know, Maryland would have seceded, but was prevented from doing so by Lincoln. Many prominent people who were known to be Southern sympathizers were jailed for no reason other than to confine them. And there were whole units that were Southern, and others that joined the Union army. Baltimore was essentially a city under occupation. It will be a long time before people forget this war."

"I know that is certainly true, Charles. I know I won't soon forget it."

Their conversation then turned to other matters. They spoke of the development of the western territories and laughed at how everyone seemed to want to be a cowboy.

"You know, I have heard that in the West, people are not judged by where they come from, the color of their skin, or even their sex. No one cares anything about you—they only want to know what you can do!" he exclaimed.

"And I've read about the strange clothes those cowboys wear!" exclaimed Martha. "Floppy vests, leather chaps, tight pants, fancy boots, and wide-brimmed hats! It sounds like the men have taken over the fashion world," she said with a laugh.

"And now we have all these new Spanish words to learn: lariat, chaps, rodeo, sombrero. How do you like my lingo?" Martha could not resist asking.

"I like it very much, señorita," he parried.

"Who are Wild Bill Hickok and Calamity Jane?" asked Martha, already off on another tangent. "And how did they get such strange names?"

"Well, people say Wild Bill has the 'fastest draw in the West' and can shoot the hat off a man and keep it in the air with bullets, and when it finally drops, the hat is rimmed with a circle of bullet holes. Now, Martha, I don't know how true that is, but it sounds good." Charles laughed. "And Calamity Jane, well, people say she can make up some tall tales and ride a horse like a man. As an author, I'm sure you know what 'calamity' means, don't you? Well, people say it fits her to a tee!"

The conversation turned to people nearer to their

hearts. Martha inquired about her stepmother and sister, Theresa, who had also moved to Maryland. Charles spoke of his wife, Rebecca, and told her how much they were enjoying life in the small town of Elkton. He encouraged Martha to consider moving there, where she would be away from the noisy city and closer to immediate family.

It was decided that he would come again in a few weeks and that they—and other family members—would visit the Centennial Exposition to be held in Philadelphia in honor of the hundredth anniversary of the signing of the Declaration of Independence.

* * * * *

June of 1876 found the Finley family, along with about ten million other people, touring the first successful world's fair ever held in America. The exposition crowds were amazed at the moving, working models of new machines—like the continuous-web printing press, the self-binding reaper, the typewriter, and Thomas Edison's duplex telegraph. Scientists were praising the work of Alexander Graham Bell, who had invented some sort of speaking device he called a telephone. Martha found the Exposition exciting, but tiring. She was glad to spend time with her relatives, but there had been too many people at the fair, she decided. On the other hand, there had been so many new things to see and think about. And she couldn't get the thought of the typewriter out of her mind.

Soon after, Martha decided to make a trip to Elkton, Maryland, as Charles had suggested. Rebecca, too, when she visited during the Exposition, had urged her to come. She had reminded Martha that there were no crowds in Elkton. Perhaps it was simply a matter of timing, but Martha was ready enough to leave Philadelphia behind—for a short time, at any rate. She wanted to see for herself what some of her relatives were talking about when they spoke so highly of their little village.

Arriving in Elkton, she at once fell in love with its quaintness, its quietness, and the friendliness of its inhabitants.

"There are so many churches!" she exclaimed to Charles. "There is almost one on every corner."

Charles, Rebecca, and Martha's stepmother endeavored to show her all the pleasures of living in a small community. She attended church with them, and was introduced to the minister and members of the congregation. Rebecca took her for walks through the town and down to the paths along Big Elk Creek, which meandered like a playful child through the sleepy little village. She enjoyed buggy rides through the surrounding countryside, her family pointing out spots of interest along the way. Her stepmother even invited the schoolmistress to tea so that Martha could meet her.

And as the weather was perfect for such outings, the family took her on picnics. Their favorite spot was a large grassy space on the creek bank that was bordered by wild berry bushes, honeysuckle, and tall maple trees.

As Martha sat on a large blanket beside the creek, dipping her toes into the clear, cool water, she remembered the time so long ago when she and her friend Carrie had taken off their shoes and stockings and dipped their toes into the little pool in the garden of her childhood home in South Bend. Laughing aloud at the sweet memory—and at that moment feeling very much like the young girl she once had been—she told her stepmother of the tête-à-tête she and Carrie had had the evening of her sixteenth birthday, confiding that she had been quite the proper hostess until Carrie had taken off her shoes and stockings. She related their discussion of some of the fashionable ladies who had attended the party—how they had thought them so old, at twenty-five and thirty—and their schoolgirl anticipation about the future.

"In a way it looks like you have come full circle, Martha," said her stepmother tenderly. "You've been out in the big world, you've supported yourself as well as you could, and allowed yourself to be taken care of. You have grown strong in many ways, and although your body hasn't always behaved itself as you might like, your physical trials have made you a more compassionate and patient person. Now that you have found a measure of success in following your heart's desire, perhaps this is the place in which to settle down. Charles is devoted to you, and so is Rebecca. I will enjoy having you near more than I can tell you." She paused, and then said, "Of course, we all know that no one can make up your mind for you. We will abide by whatever decision you make."

"I appreciate that, Mama," said Martha with a smile, "but it must be obvious to all of you that I have fallen in love with this lovely place—the quiet, the peace, and of course, this happy little creek that soothes my soul—and also my toes," she finished with an impish grin, making gentle splashes in the water with her feet.

And after enjoying her relatives and Elkton's charming atmosphere for a week, Martha decided there wasn't a thing she didn't like about it, and determined to make it her home.

Chapter Ten

MOVING AGAIN

"I HAVE DECIDED to move to Elkton, Maryland," announced Martha to her sister Eleanor the day after her return from her visit. They were sitting in the kitchen snapping the beans Eleanor had just picked from her small garden.

"Whatever for?" was Eleanor's quick reply. "I know how you hate the stress of moving. And Elkton is quite a distance away."

"It is only about fifty miles south, just over the Delaware line. Since you've visited there, you know what a quaint little village it is. Being close to mama and Charles and his family would be nice, and I would like to know Rebecca better. They haven't been married very long, you know," said Martha. "I'm thinking of having a house built there—now that I can finally take care of myself," she concluded.

Her sister chuckled as she set the table for their supper. "Well, I will say no more against the move. I know well enough that when you get a notion to do something, it is almost impossible to talk you out of it."

"Eleanor, it seems quite practical to me. We have other relatives besides Charles and Mama living in Elkton. I'd like to have a home of my own, and now the Lord has made it possible for me to do that. Please be happy for me," she said softly. "I'll write often and we can visit back and forth. And perhaps, if I move down there I can get away from those relatives here who still chide me about my 'frivolous storytelling,' " she said with a laugh. "You and Mary and Elizabeth—and many others—have taken care of me in various ways for a long time. Now I am not only able to take care of myself, I am in a position at last to help others. I want to give back what God has given me."

Having decided upon the move, Martha began making the necessary arrangements to transport her books and personal effects to her stepmother's home in Elkton, where she would live until her own house was built. Reflecting upon her other moves, Martha decided that what she had disliked about them was that she had never had the sense that she was moving to a place she would make her permanent home. This time it was different, and this time she was excited about her new adventure—until she started packing and realized how much she had accumulated over the years! Determined that even the packing would not be tiresome this time, Martha enlisted the help of her nieces.

"Oh, Aunt Martha, what are you going to do with all these books?" wailed Margaret. "We're going to need at least five crates!"

"I've ordered them already. They should arrive tomorrow. In the meantime, we can pack the china in the small crate that's on the back porch. And Catherine, you can come help me with the linens," she said, carrying a pile of sheets into her bedroom, Margaret's younger sister following at her heels.

"Aunt Martha, we're going to miss you terribly," sighed Catherine, as she obediently folded the heavy linen sheets and placed them in the trunk at the end of the bed.

' "Well, my dear, as soon as my house is built you shall pay me a visit and stay as long as your mama can spare you. There will be plenty of room for you and Margaret, and half a dozen of your cousins as well! I've rarely lived alone, and I'm sure I will enjoy the visits of all who come to see me."

Upon her arrival in Elkton, Martha settled in with her stepmother, enjoying the opportunity to be near her once again. At the same time, she was eager to get her new house underway. Charles had found a large lot on Main Street, and she had made a special trip to Elkton to see it. Since it had suited her perfectly (as Charles had thought it would) she had made a deposit on the property at once, leaving Charles to finalize the purchase. She was looking forward to having a hand in its design, and was enjoying the thought that at last she could have everything just the way she wanted it.

So before a week had passed, Martha made an appointment with a local contractor Charles had recommended, and the two sat down to go over house plans.

Mr. Logan had brought a portfolio of house plans, and Martha was examining them one by one.

"I know I want a three-story house with large rooms and windows—lots and lots of windows. I love large, airy rooms, and I want to be able to see the street from the windows. This one might do very well," she said, holding up one of the plans so they could both look at it.

Mr. Logan smiled at this high-spirited lady who was acting like a school child. He wondered briefly if all famous writers were as eccentric as Miss Finley, and then turned his attention back to the matter at hand. She had finished discussing the windows and now she was describing the kind of porch she wanted.

"And sir, it must have a large verandah, just like the one in this plan." She indicated another design. "I do so love sitting on the verandah in the evening," she told him exuberantly. "I'll have a porch swing. Oh yes, I want a porch swing."

"Of course, Miss Finley," said Mr. Logan with a smile.

And so they discussed the details of Martha's dream house. Or rather, Martha told the builder what she wanted, and Mr. Logan smiled, agreed to her specifications, and took copious notes. He was glad he had brought his portfolio, as the different house designs seemed to help Miss Finley get a clear picture of what the house would look like. But he still had a lot of work to do, he realized, because to build the house she described to him, he would need to use parts of several of the designs he had brought. She had a good eye for design, too, he decided. Everything she requested was feasible, and the proportions of the house she envisioned were pleasing. The house would be one-of-a-kind, and he was glad, for it would be a pleasure to build.

"Please don't cut down any of the large trees," Martha requested. "I love trees, and those on the lot will provide wonderful shade in the summer."

The builder continued to make notes. "Yes, Miss Finley."

"When the house is finished, I'm going to plant lilac bushes all along the side of the house," she added, almost to herself.

"Yes, Miss Finley," said Mr. Logan, acquiescing out of habit.

"Mr. Logan, how soon can you get started?" asked Martha, when she had at last made known all her requests. The eyes behind the thick spectacles were bright with anticipation, and the small face that looked up at him was aglow with happiness.

"Very soon. First I must draw up the plans, which will take several days. And then, I have one other project to complete before I begin on your house. I will call on you at the beginning of next week. By then I will be able to give you a starting date, and give you some idea about when you can expect to move into your new house," he responded.

True to his word, at their next meeting Mr. Logan gave Martha a schedule for the construction of the house. They discussed the cost of the project, and it was agreed that Martha would pay Mr. Logan $2.25 a day and supply all the building materials. Thus the work began.

* * * * * *

Spring arrived, carried on on the winds and rains of March. Winter's icy breath was gone. Gentle breezes were in the air. Crocuses had been blooming for weeks, and the daffodils were in bud everywhere. The trees held faint tinges of yellow-green, and violets were showing their pretty faces along the roadside. The air was full of pleasant sounds: insects were chirping and birds were twittering.

Martha was awake at dawn, beside herself with anticipation. Today was the day she was to move into her new house at 259 East Main Street! Dressing quickly, she put a light shawl over the practical navy blue dress she had selected for the occasion—reluctantly leaving on its hook her new flowered silk with the blue trim. There would be a lot to do today, she knew, and she could wear the silk when she held her housewarming. Downstairs, Martha and her stepmother shared a light breakfast.

"Oh, Mama, I'm too excited to eat," said Martha, putting down her muffin. "I can't believe I'm actually going to live in my own house!"

"I know it is a big day for you, Martha. I am very happy for you—although I will miss having you here with me," she told her stepdaughter. "And you aren't really so far away, after all—and you're much closer than you were in Pennsylvania!"

"That's right, Mama. I will be able to see you every day," said Martha with a smile as she rose from the table. "I'd like to go over to the house by myself, before the others get there. Do you mind? I just want to see the house as it is before all the furniture is put around and it is filled up with my books."

"Not at all, dear. I will be happy to come with Charles and Rebecca, and we'll all help you with the unpacking," responded Mrs. Finley.

"Thank you for understanding, Mama," Martha said, kissing her stepmother lightly on the cheek.

It was a short ride from her stepmother's house to 259 East Main Street. Once there, Martha paused for a moment, gazing at her new home. In front of the house a neat hedge had been planted; in years to come it would become an attractive trim along the edge of the street. The lilac bushes she had wanted had been planted just last week. The leaves on the trees that Martha had been so insistent on keeping were just beginning to uncurl, and there was a pale green tinge all around the house. And tomorrow, the pansies will be planted, she thought to herself.

Stepping down from the small carriage, one of America's most famous authors picked up her long skirts, moved up the walk as sedately as her excitement would allow, climbed the front steps, and walked through the front door of her new house. Though considered a cottage, in reality Martha's home was quite large, especially for one person. It contained a library, two parlors, a dining room, a kitchen, a conservatory, and four bedrooms. A beautiful staircase led to the rooms on the second floor. Although she had first thought of using an upstairs bedroom as her writing room, Martha had decided to use the library instead, where she would be surrounded by her books. Also, she loved the large windows on the first floor. They were just what she had requested, and they provided the room with lots of light and fresh air.

Martha walked through the empty rooms, enjoying the stillness and the cool spring breeze that came in through the open windows. Very shortly, she knew, the house would be in a flurry of activity. She stood at her bedroom window and gave thanks to the One who had always looked after her, the One who had always provided for her and sustained her. She asked for wisdom and discernment in her writing, and strength that she would be able to share with others in her life and through her writing the great gifts she had received from God.

"If I can help them learn to trust God, and see what He will do, I will have done much," she murmured.

Knowing she would be unable to do much of the furniture arranging herself, she had recruited Charles and Rebecca to help her. They were due to arrive shortly with her stepmother, whose impeccable taste would be invaluable in all questions of interior design.

Amid the chaos that prevailed a few hours later, Martha reflected that she had been right to have had her morning moment of quiet. The moving men had come with the furniture, crates, and books. Much of what arrived had been newly purchased, because never before had Martha had a house of her own. She had had no room for, and no need for, a houseful of furniture, kitchen equipment, or rugs and drapes. Although the items had been placed in their designated rooms, there was still much work to be done. Charles placed the furniture at her direction, and Rebecca washed the windows, hung the curtains, and arranged the contents of the kitchen cabinets. Mrs. Finley helped as she was able. Martha placed her writing materials in her desk, and arranged her many books on the library shelves. Her kerosene lamps were set about to provide good lighting during the long evenings.

She and Charles were discussing the placement of the dining room furniture, when Rebecca entered the room carrying a small box.

"Martha," she exclaimed, "look what I've just unearthed from the crate of kitchen supplies!" She placed the box on the dining room table and, opening the lid, took out a beautifully crafted brass bell. "It's quite lovely," she continued, "but whatever is it for?"

"Oh, I plan to use it to summon the maid," said Martha calmly.

"But Martha, you don't have a maid!" interjected Charles.

"Well," laughed his sister, "I'm going to get one."

"My, my, such notions you have," he teased. "But you're right, I think a companion-housekeeper is a grand idea. I don't like the idea of you living here alone—not that you'll be alone for long. It seems you have a long line of nieces anxious to pay you a visit," he said, smiling mischievously. "That is quite an impressive corner cupboard you have there," he added. "Is that new china?"

"It is! Do you like it?"

"Very much. It even matches the colors in the room," he said with a laugh.

"We're both very glad you approve, since we picked it out together," said Rebecca, with a grin. "And now, I must return to my cupboards." And she hurried off in the direction of the kitchen.

Charles looked at everything, inside and out. He was impressed with the large verandah and its intriguing lattice work, encircling half the house and adding dimension to her "cottage." He appreciated the many upstairs dormers that gave a wonderful view of the front lawn. He had even noticed the flowers already planted along the front walk.

Finally, after a long afternoon of setting Martha's house in order, it was time for Mrs. Finley, Charles, and Rebecca to return home. Embracing his sister, and then holding her at arm's length, Charles proclaimed, "Martha Finley, one of the most famous authors in America, you have one of the grandest homes in Elkton. And I learned from Mama today that you have just become a member of New York's prestigious Authors' Club. Congratulations!" And he made her a sweeping bow.

"Thank you, brother. And I thank all of you for helping me put my house together today. I couldn't have done it without you," said Martha, with feeling.

"It was our pleasure, Martha dear," said her sister-in-law. "And don't forget the cold potato pie and chicken we left for your supper."

"No, Rebecca, I won't. It was wonderful of you to think of it," said Martha with a smile.

From the front door Martha waved good-bye to her family. Laughing and waving back, the three departed for home. Charles handed his mother into the small carriage Martha had brought over in the morning, then settled Rebecca in their own, and Martha turned and went back into her house, tired but happy. A leisurely tour of her now furnished house gave her quiet satisfaction. Everything was arranged to perfection. She would have her potato pie and chicken with a cup of tea and go straight to bed, she decided. It had been a long, but happy, day.

* * * * *

Resting for a moment by an open window in the library, Martha smelled the faint, sweet scent of the honeysuckle that grew along one side of her yard. The lone dogwood, a few short weeks ago thick with blooms, was rapidly shedding its white beauties. The summer heat was fast approaching.

She had known that with such a large home, and her problems with her eyesight, she would need domestic help. Two weeks ago she had placed an ad in the local newspaper, the *Cecil Whig*, for a housekeeper. She hoped to find someone who was a good housekeeper, and who was loyal and dependable as well. If only she could find someone like Dora, her mother's house-keeper in Indiana, she mused. Dora had been almost a member of the family until she left to care for her aging mother.

A knock at the door brought Martha out of her reverie. Hastening to open it, Martha found herself face to face with a tall, solidly-built individual about her own age, who had large blue eyes, pale skin, and a mat-ter-of-fact, no-nonsense expression. The woman was dressed plainly, but her clothes were very neat. Looking back on this meeting later, Martha reflected that the only hint she had of Mary White's boundless energy and irrepressible personality were the red curls that just wouldn't quite stay put under her brown bonnet.

"Miss Finley?"

"Yes, I am Miss Finley. How may I help you?"

"Miss Finley, my name is Mary White. I read your advertisement in the paper for a housekeeper and I've come to apply for the job. The lady I recently kept house for went to live with her son, and I'm presently between situations, as they say."

Martha, amused by the woman's straightforward manner, was nevertheless pleased. "Please come in," she said.

Following Martha into the front hall, Mary White continued her speech. Handing Martha the papers she held in her hand, she said, "These are my references, ma'am. I'm a thorough church-goer, I read my Bible, and do my prayin' every day. I can dust, clean, polish, sweep, wash, mend, and just about anything else you might need." Martha thought this was an answer to prayer, indeed. Martha escorted her prospective housekeeper into the library, where they spent the good part of the afternoon discussing Martha's needs and Mary's qualifications. Martha sent Charles a note the very next day, and together they checked Mary's references and discussed her suitability.

In a week's time, Mary White was settling into her responsibilities as Martha's housekeeper. She soon became much more than a housekeeper, caring for Martha like a sister and bringing an energy into the big house that became a great blessing to Martha, particularly at those times when she was not well.

One morning, after the breakfast things had been put away and Mary had organized her work for the day, she approached Martha in the library where she was working at her writing desk.

"Miss Finley," she began in her brisk, autocratic way, "I know what a busy and important author you are. I don't want you to worry about a thing in this house. I will make sure that everything is taken care of. You go right on with your writing and I will take care of everything else."

Martha smiled. "Thank you, Mary. I have every confidence that I am in the best of hands." She paused, then said casually, "And by the way, Mary, you may call me Martha if you wish."

"No, ma'am, if you please, I prefer to address you as Miss Finley. You are my employer, and it wouldn't be respectful to call you anything else," responded Mary with firmness.

"Very well, Miss Finley it is," agreed Martha.

In the months that followed Martha came to realize that she was indeed in excellent hands. The vigorous, bossy, red-headed housekeeper soon became indispensable to her not only as a housekeeper, but as a companion as well.

Martha had many callers. Martha's stepmother, sisters, nieces and nephews, and other relatives as well, all came to wish her well and to see her new house. Friends called from the Presbyterian church Martha attended, all wanting to see her grand new home.

June and July passed quickly. Martha's pen was never idle. Often she would have to stop, rub her eyes, and look away for a while before being able to focus again. She was very thankful for her glasses, and admitted to Mary that she did not know what she would do without them.

Young readers were calling for more Elsie adventures. Martha, as always, spent a great deal of time in research. Often she would look up from her work and see the crisp, starched-white curtains billowing in the breeze by the open windows, and reminded thereby of Mary's impeccable housekeeping and unceasing care of her, a smile would come to her lips and she would offer up a silent thanksgiving to God for her many blessings.

* * * * * *

In 1876, Martha had finished *Elsie's Motherhood*. A year later *Elsie's Children* was in the hands of her readers. Six books recounting the adventures of Elsie Dinsmore had been published. As six volumes was the usual number in a series at that time, Martha wanted to stop. She even wrote "The series closes." The Elsie books were being called one of the first series for American girls.

The year 1878 brought great sadness to the Finley family. Little Helen, the first-born daughter of Charles and Rebecca Finley, passed away. She was only seven years old. Martha had spent much time with her, telling her stories of her days as a schoolteacher, and joining in her childish pleasures. She gave her brother and his wife what comfort she could.

Mildred Keith, the first of the Mildred books—a companion series about one of Elsie's cousins—was published in this same year. Still another novel—*Signing the Contract*—was published in 1879, but it received little attention. It was Elsie that readers demanded to read more about, so Martha complied. In 1880, the year Martha celebrated her fifty-second birthday, *Elsie's Widowhood* was published.

Some readers complained. "Why does Elsie have to become a widow?" they asked. In fact, it was Martha's publishers who had demanded that she bury Mr. Travilla! They argued that the most fundamental aspect of the saga of *Elsie Dinsmore* was her relationship with her father, and felt that that emphasis should be maintained.

In the preface to *Elsie's Widowhood*, Martha wrote,

It was not in my heart to give to my favorite child, Elsie, the sorrows of widowhood. But the public made the title and demanded the book; and the public, I am told, is autocratic. So what could I do but write the story and try to show how the love of Christ in the heart can make life happy even under sore bereavement? The apostle says, "I am filled with comfort, I am exceeding joyful in all our tribulation"; and since trouble, trial and affliction are the lot of all in this world of sin and sorrow, what greater kindness could I do you, dear reader, than to show you where to go for relief and consolation? That this little book may teach the sweet lesson to many a tried and burdened soul, is the earnest prayer of your friend.

At this time numerous newspaper articles were written about Martha, and reporters were writing to ask for interviews. She was called "one of the leading authors of all time." In addition to The Elsie Dinsmore books, she had written many children's books over the years. There were nine volumes in The Do Good Library series, six in The Little Books for Little Readers series, and eleven in The Pewit's Nest series.

But in the midst of all the fame, Martha managed to keep her life very private. Most of her time was spent at her writing, at church, and with family and friends.

* * * * *

It was a hot day. Martha went into the kitchen for some iced tea. Mary was out doing the day's marketing. A huge block of ice had been delivered that morning, and Martha began chipping away at it for some small pieces to cool her drink.

"I wonder what this new refrigerator machine I've heard so much about is really like," she mused to herself. "Maybe I'll look into it. Someone said it can make its own ice. I'd sure like to see that!"

Chipping away at the big block of ice, Martha's thoughts went back to that cold winter day so long ago when her father had taken her to the pond to watch the workers cut ice to store for the summer. She remembered watching in fascination as the men scraped the ice clear of snow and dirt. A machine called a marker had gone out onto the ice and had begun to cut grooves up and down about three feet apart. She recalled how frightened she had been, fearing the ice would break and the men fall into the deep cold water.

"Don't be fearful, daughter," her father had said soothingly. "Those men know what they're doing. And besides, the ice is probably two or three feet thick."

Amazed, she had watched the process. When they had finished cutting parallel grooves in one direction, the men turned at a ninety degree angle and worked their way across the pond, making perpendicular grooves the same distance apart. Her father explained that this was what made the blocks of ice. Then a plow-with a steel bar fitted with sharp knives-cut the grooves even deeper to loosen the ice blocks. Finally, the blocks floated to shore through channels in the ice.

On shore, she had watched as the ice blocks were slid up a slanting board into an ice house and packed in sawdust. Father had explained that the ice house was insulated to keep out heat and reduce melting.

Finally Martha had enough chips for her tea. As she stirred it, she remembered how cold she had been standing there, but recalled also enjoying the warm relationship she had enjoyed with her father, and how she had not wanted to leave because time with him was so special. Oh, how she still missed him!

Returning to the library, Martha went back to her desk. Still lost in thoughts of the past, she lightly traced the painted roses on the globe of the lamp that stood on her writing table. It had been her mother's favorite. She was planning to have gas lamps installed all over the house very soon, but she knew she'd never give away this kerosene lamp, with its roses and memories of times long past.

Chapter Eleven

STRIKING OUT AT INDEPENDENCE

MARTHA WANTED TO TAKE ANOTHER TRIP—this time to the Midwest. Worried about her poor eyesight, her family did not want her to go. For her part, she did not hesitate to remind her family that most of her problems came when she sat writing, which she would not be doing on her trip. And as she had just bought herself a new pair of eyeglasses with stronger lenses, she was quite confident in her ability to make the journey. In the end, however, she agreed to allow her brother Charles to travel with her.

Some time before, on Charles' advice, Martha had bought a half ownership in a bakery in Chicago. Not only was she interested in seeing for herself the nature of her investment, but she was also interested in purchasing some real estate in Kansas. She greatly valued Charles' point of view on financial matters, and since he was in the banking and investment business and had become her guide in her business ventures, his presence on the trip would actually be quite welcome.

Train accommodations had greatly improved since Martha's first trip to Washington, D. C., and she and Charles made this trip in style, reserving spaces on one of Pullman's Palace Cars. These had comfortable seats which converted into beds, thereby allowing her to get more rest—at least this was one of her winning arguments against those who advised against the long trip.

"My, isn't this wonderful!" exclaimed Martha to her brother. "This is much different from the trip Papa and Mama and Amy and I made to Washington, D. C., so many years ago."

"I'm sure it is. And do you know that these comfortable seats actually convert into beds?" asked Charles. "We'll be able to get a lot more rest than you did on your previous trip."

The two had not invested in a sleeping car, however. A sleeper would have cost around $100, which was more than the average working man earned in a month and a great luxury, even for Martha in her now relatively secure financial position.

Martha thought the wood paneling, the reading lamps, the carpeting, and even the mirrors were beautiful. The train attendants fussed over her. In the luxurious dining car, their table was covered with gleaming white cloths and the food was served very hot. There was even an organ, and she and Charles enjoyed listening as some of the passengers spent time singing around the instrument. Charles was an attentive and enjoyable companion. His full beard, well-tailored clothes, and air of confidence were the source of many admiring and curious glances by other passengers. Yes, Charles was very distinguished, Martha decided. In fact, he reminded her a lot of their father. Moreover, it was a delight to be going on this adventure with him!

In Chicago, Charles and Martha visited her bakery. Though most women still baked their own bread, the bakery had many customers among the wealthier residents and the better restaurants. Many different kinds of bread and rolls were baked daily and distributed all over the city. Martha watched as golden loaves came out of the large ovens, and enjoyed the aroma of freshly baked bread. After learning step by step the process of commercial bread baking—which was very much like baking bread at home, only on a much larger scale—and talking with the manager and the workers, she concluded that her investment was in good hands. Thus satisfied, she and Charles boarded the train for Kansas to see about her real estate venture.

While traveling, the two discussed the wisdom of investing in the Scott Fertilizer Company and the James F. Powers Foundry Company of Cecil County—the county in which Elkton was situated. Charles concluded, "I do not believe you can go wrong investing in these two local companies, Martha. I will look into it for you when we get back."

When they returned home a few weeks later, Martha was completely worn out, and took to her bed for a few days' rest. The long trip had depleted her energies a little too much. Her family of course chided her greatly for not having taken better care of herself and tried to blame Charles for her ill health. Martha, however, insisted that he was not to blame, saying that she had paid no attention to his attempts to get her to rest on the journey. Even Mary went about with an air of "I told you so." But Martha didn't care. Her independence had won out, and she was very willing to pay the penalty for her overexertion. She would never forget all the wonderful experiences she had had on her trip. She returned to her writing with the images and experiences of her Midwestern trip still in her mind.

* * * * *

One day, Martha's niece Catherine arrived from Philadelphia for an extended visit. Catherine was the second daughter of Martha's sister Elizabeth. She and Martha corresponded regularly, and Martha had been looking forward to her visit. The Finleys were a large family and Martha had many nieces and nephews.

Catherine was a lovely young lady of twenty-one who had blue eyes, a mouth that was usually turned up in a smile, and a cheerful personality. It was a beautiful sunny day without a hint of a cloud in the sky, and Catherine looked as lovely as a picture in her white muslin dress trimmed with blue and pink ribbon and her straw broad-brimmed hat trimmed in ribbons of the same colors. Her long blond hair was piled up under the hat—except for the wisps that the light breeze gently untucked and danced with—and her cheeks were pink with excitement, Martha noticed.

"What a fashionable young lady you have become, my dear!" exclaimed Martha as she gave her niece a hug. "Why only yesterday you were running in the meadow gathering daisies, and overnight you have turned into an elegant stranger! And a matching parasol, too! Truly you are a sight for these poor eyes."

Catherine glowed with pleasure, and answered, "Thank you, Aunt Martha. I wanted to look especially nice when I came to visit you." Remembering how she had pleaded with Mama to let her have the parasol, she was very happy Aunt Martha had remarked on it.

A short while later they were enjoying a cup of tea in the front parlor. Catherine noticed the beautiful lace curtains at the tall windows overlooking the street.

"Aunt Martha, those are lovely lace curtains," Catherine exclaimed admiringly. "The design is quite unusual." Laughing, she continued, "Do you remember years ago when my mother took down her mail-order curtains to wash them? They were so limp and shapeless. They even hung lopsided."

"Yes, I remember," said Martha, taking a sip of tea. "I remember how upset she was. They had been so stiff and grand when she first put them up."

"Remember the dear neighbor lady who stopped over and saw mama crying? 'A little starch, Ma'am,' she said, 'a little starch and a little stretching. That's all you need. It'll fix those laces right up again. Those curtains are made of cotton, so you must starch each time you wash them. When they are still wet, you've got to stretch, stretch, stretch.' "

"Yes, dear, I remember the whole thing. That was a long time ago." mused Martha. "I guess we all learned a lesson that day."

"Aunt Martha," said Catherine, "tell me about your health. You don't mention it in your letters, but I get tidbits from Aunt Rebecca. How is your eyesight? I would imagine that all this writing puts a great deal of strain on you." There was concern in her voice.

Martha didn't like to talk about herself, and evaded the subject whenever possible. "Well, Catherine, my eyesight isn't the best, but I take my time when I am writing. When I feel strained, or I think a headache is coming on, I rest for a while. I do lie down more frequently than I used to. If I sit too long my back aches—I suppose from the time I fell. I do try to take care of myself," Martha said in an offhanded way. "It's really nothing to worry about. As you see, I am doing quite well."

Changing the subject, Martha continued, "Would you like to take a walk down by Big Elk Creek? It's a lovely day, and a fine opportunity to show off your new finery. Many residents of our little town enjoy strolling by the cool stream on days like this."

"Oh, that sounds lovely!" exclaimed Catherine. "I am ready to go whenever you say the word."

Martha rang for Mary and asked her to prepare a picnic lunch for them. As Mary returned to the kitchen to fulfill her employer's request, Martha added to Catherine, "I know you will love it at the creek. It's almost my favorite place to go in Elkton. And besides," she said conspiratorially, "I know a lovely little spot where we can very unobtrusively dip our toes in the water."

Catherine was speechless. Her old auntie was behaving like a girl of sixteen! Laughing silently, she said to herself, "I wonder if Mama knows Aunt Martha is so unconventional! But maybe that is why she says I remind her so much of my Aunt Martha."

The lunch was soon ready, and the two ladies were off—parasols, blanket, and picnic basket in hand. Walking along, Catherine said, "I read in the newspaper last week that you have twenty-five million readers. That is incredible!" She looked at her aunt, who had a sweet, calm expression on her face, and thought to herself what strong sentiments were hidden beneath that kind visage.

"Frankly, Aunt Martha," she went on in her outspoken way, "I don't know how you have gotten away with some of the things you have written through the years. It amazes me how all those strong political feelings you have given some of your characters don't seem to bother anyone." She arched her eyebrows and shook her head. "And——what you have said about slavery, and the Christian faith! All through your books you refer to God as being the most important person in whom one can trust. Most people don't want to hear that these days."

Martha laughed easily. "Well, my dear niece, those are things I believe in. I feel I must express them."

"I know you are an advocate of education and opportunities for women," Catherine continued, "but I'm surprised that there's been no negative reaction to your writing about it. For instance, the statement you made—or should I say, Elsie made, that she was not 'bringing up daughters to consider marriage as the chief end of a woman.' Really, Aunt Martha, that is pretty strong," Catherine insisted, with a smile. "Also one of your other characters said, 'I'm the most unfortunate woman—the poorest in the whole country—I wasn't brought up to support myself.' Honestly, you've surprised even me!"

"Catherine, there are still many who think that girls should concentrate only on music, needlework, and painting. Some men even say that a woman's brain is smaller and can't learn as much as a man's. And—you know how difficult it is for a woman to get into college. Even now a woman gets paid half as much as a man for doing the same job. As an author I am often criticized by men because of my womanly writings.

"But what about you? I'm tired of talking about myself. Tell me what is going on in your life. Do you have any beaux?" asked Martha. Have you 'set your cap' for anyone yet?"

"No, not yet, Aunt Martha. Some people say I am too picky—that I want someone just perfect. There was quite a dashing young man who paid over $5.00 for my pie at the church social last month. I was pleasantly surprised, having never seen him before. He just started bidding, smiling at me all the while. And you know, when someone buys your pie you do have to share it with him over supper—that's the rule. He did have the prettiest eyes," Catherine prattled on. "Then he came to call, and after a few weeks, papa found he wasn't the person we thought. I told him I wasn't allowed to see him anymore."

Martha chuckled. She always enjoyed hearing of her nieces' adventures.

The green banks of Big Elk Creek were very inviting, and Martha led her niece unerringly to her favorite spot. "Just the right place for a picnic," she said happily. "And look downstream a little. There are some young people dipping their toes into the water. It looks like we aren't the only ones with the right idea." Catherine carefully placed the basket on a level spot of ground and helped her aunt spread the blanket under a large maple tree whose branches on the creek side nearly touched the water. Martha said a quiet blessing, and Catherine served the picnic lunch.

For awhile they ate in a companionable silence that was interrupted only by exclamations of pleasure over the treats prepared for them by Mary. Then Martha spoke casually, a quaint smile on her lips. "Catherine, I've been thinking about stopping the Elsie series. What do you think about that? There are now ten books in it, and I think that might be enough."

"What? Stop the Elsie series! Oh, I don't know about that, Aunt Martha. I don't think your little readers would be very happy," her niece said decisively. "You know what happened last time you got such a notion."

"I really don't know what to do," responded her aunt. "I know I've allowed some of my characters to be very outspoken, but I believe that women should have more freedom. I may be unmarried, self-supporting, and famous, but I'm also subjected to many situations uncommon to most women." Then, with steel determination in her voice, she added, "Now, I'm going to tell you something that will really shock you. Brace yourself."

"Oh Aunt Martha, what now? If you are not careful, you'll be run out of town!"

"No, Catherine, this is very serious. I have hired a lawyer and am taking my publishers to court."

"What?" gasped her niece. "What do you mean, you're taking your publishers to court? Oh, auntie, you can't do that! A lady just doesn't do things like that! What will the family say?"

Stubbornly Martha replied, "It has nothing to do with being a lady. It has to do with what is right. Dodd, Mead have continuously refused to give me the copyright to my Elsie series. You already know that, as we have discussed it before in our letters. They are paying me just what they want for my manuscripts. I am going to get the copyright, and the publisher will have to pay me royalties. I've spoken with your Uncle Charles and I'm seeing my lawyer in the morning." Martha went back to her sandwich as if she had not just dropped a bombshell.

Martha went to court and won her case. She began to receive royalties from the sales of her books, and she became even wealthier.

On rare occasions, when Martha was seen on the streets of Elkton, passersby would whisper, "There goes Miss Finley, the lady that writes all those Elsie books. They say she is very religious, and also very rich. Why, she's probably the wealthiest lady in Elkton."

* * * * *

Martha's house ran smoothly under Mary's supervision. Through the years she became devoted to her employer, and as a consequence, often quite protective. Over time, the two became very good friends.

"Land sakes!" exclaimed Mary one afternoon, looking over Martha's shoulder as she sat at the dining room table reading the *Baltimore Sun*. "What is that?" she, asked, pointing to the photograph on the front page.

"Well," chuckled Martha, "they are calling it a skyscraper." She always enjoyed Mary's blusterings and exclamations when she didn't understand something.

"A *what*?"

"Look what it says here," continued Martha. "They're saying it will reach up into the sky—ten stories high."

"What in the world is going to hold it up? Just tell me that, Miss Finley! Why it will fall right over, you just mark my words!" interrupted Mary. "I never heard of such a thing! Why don't men learn to keep their feet on the ground?" she muttered as she huffed out into the kitchen.

But Martha read on, interested as always in the inventions and events of her time. She learned that the world's first skyscraper, the Home Insurance Building, was being built in Chicago. Even in 1884, limited space and the high cost of land were causing architects and builders to think of going upwards rather than out-wards. Out in the kitchen, Mary was still muttering that no one would ever catch her in one of those "shaky things" that would rock every time the wind blew.

The next year, Martha's Elsie Dinsmore faced some competition for the hearts of her young readers. Mark Twain, riverboat pilot and journalist turned author, renowned for his short stories and travel journals, completed his masterpiece, *Huckleberry Finn*. "Huck," that mischievous, lovable boy of the Mississippi River, was to become an enduring character in American fiction. In this same year *Elsie at Nantucket* and *Mildred at Home* went into the hands of Martha's readers.

Not quite two years later, three more books were published: *Thorn in the Nest*, *Mildred's Boys and Girls*, and *Elsie's Kith and Kin*. Her literary pen was never at rest.

Chapter Twelve

GOD CARES ABOUT LITTLE THINGS

MARTHA'S HAIR WAS now grey, almost white. She had grown slightly plump over the years. The neighborhood children thought of her as a sweet little lady. She was warm and kind, with a cheerful smile and a twinkle in her eye. When they discovered that she could tell an exciting story as well as write one, the little ones began gathering on her verandah, asking to hear a story. This was a favorite time for her also, and after bidding them to sit down and quiet themselves, she would begin.

One late afternoon she announced, in her best school teacher voice, "My story is called 'God Cares For Little Things.' Now listen carefully, because I'm going to ask some questions at the end.

"An old Scottish man walked down a dirt road. He had no buggy, no cart, and no horse; so he had to walk wherever he went. His back was bent and his hair was white. People called him 'Old Scotty,' and he always had a smile on his face. He loved God with all his heart and liked to watch God answer his prayers.

"Old Scotty was on his way to another town to hear a camp meeting preacher. Thankful for two good feet, he sang awhile, prayed awhile, and quoted Bible verses as he walked along. Soon he became tired, and sat down on a rock, knowing there was time because he had started out early. Shortly thereafter, a young man came walking briskly along.

" 'Good afternoon,' said the youth.

" 'Good afternoon to you, my young fellow. Where might ye be going?'

" 'Oh, I'm going to the next town to hear a famous man of the gospel. I'm going to be a preacher myself. This man is one of the greatest of our day!' said the young man excitedly.

" 'Well, is he now? I just happen to be goin' there myself. Do you mind if I be walkin' along with ye?'

"The young man acquiesced graciously, and the two new friends had much to talk about as they traveled. Soon they were hungry and, as each had brought his supper, just outside of town they sat down to eat. Old Scotty asked the young lad to say the blessing. The youth gave forth with a fancy, pious prayer of long words and lengthy sentences. Then, after the simple meal they again bowed their heads and Old Scotty prayed this time.

" 'Dear Father, now we want to thank ye for our fellowship this day. We've come a long way. We pray for ye power on the meetin' tonight—and Lord, bless this young man. He wants to be a preacher for ye. And—Father, before we go on I have a request just for me. I've some trouble and I'm askin' ye to help. You know, Lord, I can't hear well and I need a seat near the front. One more thing—I need some shoes. I've got holes in mine. Would you give me some shoes? I've no money to buy—and Lord, I'm needin' to spend the night in town and have no place to stay. Would you give me shelter tonight? Thank you, Father, I know you will. Amen.'

" 'Well, Son, we'd better be gettin' along.'

" 'Sir, do you mind if I ask a question?'

" 'Well, no Son, what is it?'

" 'Those things you prayed. Do you really think God cares and will answer? You know, God is awfully busy!'

" 'Ah-h-h, my Lord does care. You must learn to trust Him. He does care about little things.'

" 'Well, I will be anxious to see if He meets all those needs you told Him about.'

"Later, Old Scotty was leaning on the tent post in the back. The service had not started. Someone tapped him on the shoulder.

" 'Sir, there's a seat down front on the first row. Hurry, before another takes it. Go quickly,' an usher said.

"As he slipped into the chair he saw a fine lady sitting there smiling.

" 'Am I to be thankin' ye for this seat, Madam?'

" 'Well, yes, my father could not come tonight and I saw you back there. I wondered if you would be able to hear.'

"The old man sang the songs with zest and listened to the choir sing with joy. He knelt in the sawdust to pray along with the others. While he was kneeling, the young lady noticed his worn shoes.

" 'What a godly old man,' she thought. 'I'm sure he loves Jesus very much. It certainly looks like he could use a pair of new shoes.'

"After the service was over the lady asked, 'Sir, would you be needing a pair of shoes? My father has a shoe store. I'm sure he would love to help you out.'

" 'Well, thank ye, Madam, I'd be much obliged. I've been prayin' about the matter.'

"Together they walked to the shoe store. On the way, they met the young man. Old Scotty smiled, 'See ye tomorrow night, Son. I'm on my way to get a new pair of shoes,' he said with a twinkle in his eye.

" 'You are! Well, good for you! I saw you got that seat in the front, too! Well, I declare!' laughed the young man.

"Old Scotty found a pair of shoes that fit just right. As they went out the door, the lady asked him where he was spending the night. She offered to drop him off in her carriage. The old man said, 'Well, thank ye, Madam. I'm not knowin' just yet. I've been prayin' about the matter.'

" 'Then come home with Father and me. We will be delighted to have you. We have an extra room and I certainly don't want you to miss the meeting tomorrow night. What do you say?'

" 'Ah-h-h-h, my dear lady. You are so kind. You have been the answer to my prayers.' They laughed heartily together.

"That evening as they all sat by the warm fire, Old Scotty told of his requests and how God had answered each one of them. Tears came to their eyes as they talked and praised the Lord for His goodness. Coming out of the next service Old Scotty and the young man met again.

" 'Good meetin,' huh?'

" 'Yes Sir, great sermons. Good music and good praying. I see you're wearing your new shoes—mighty nice ones too. I saw you down front again too. Hey, by the way, Sir, did you get a place to—ah-h-h, I'm not even going to ask. Somehow I just know you did!'

" 'Yes, Son, I did. God cares about little things. Remember that when you get to preachin.' God cares about little things.'

"Old Scotty walked down the street in his new shoes, humming,

> Jesus loves me, this I know
> For the Bible tells me so.
> Little ones to Him belong

They are weak, but He is strong.
Yes, Jesus loves me, Yes, Jesus loves me.
Yes, Jesus loves me,
The Bible tells me so.

"And that, children, is the end of the story. Let's all sing that song together," said Martha. And so they did.

Chapter Thirteen

NEW CONTRAPTIONS

"HAVE YOU READ the morning paper yet, Miss Finley?" asked Mary, as she dusted the bookshelves. They were in the library, where Martha was researching a subject for her writing.

"Not yet, Mary, I want to finish this first. What's in the news today?"

"Why, there's an article in there about some of the big newspaper editors in the country trying to stop the publication of the Elsie books. They say they have had enough of Elsie Dinsmore. One editor has been very explicit that he wants something beside your Elsie!"

Martha smiled, more to herself than to Mary. Softly, but in a tone that revealed the determination for which she was so well-known, she responded, "As you are no doubt aware, I am not writing to please those newspaper editors. I'm writing for my young readers. As long as they are happy, I will continue to give them more adventures of our little Southern friend." She lifted her chin resolutely.

A loyal follower of Martha's fictional heroine, Mary was clearly bothered by the newspaper account. "Land sakes, Miss Finley, I just don't think it's right. It's not a bit right—them saying things like that!"

The next morning Martha was sitting at the parlor window that faced the street. "Here comes Old Dan," she said to Mary, who had come in with the morning paper. "He seems a bit slow today." Old Dan was the horse that pulled Mr. Lindell's milk cart all over town. "By the way, is milk still eight cents a quart?" asked Martha.

"Yes, ma'am, it is, but butter has gone up a little," replied Mary as she peered out the window at Old Dan. The milk cart stopped in front of the house and a young lad hopped out, carrying two quarts of milk— Martha's standing order—up on the porch. The lad's name was Joseph Grant, and it was his secret hope each morning as he delivered the milk that he would get a glimpse of the rich mysterious lady author who lived at 259 Main Street. Never once was his wish granted. It was always the housekeeper who opened the door and said "Good morning, Joseph."

Martha followed Mary as she took the milk to the kitchen. Placing the bottles carefully in the icebox, Mary commented, "I'm glad they finally decided to put milk in bottles. I didn't like those old cans."

Taking down a cup and saucer from the cupboard in preparation for her mid-morning cup of tea, Martha asked offhandedly, "What's the average pay for a milkman? Is it very much?"

"I believe it's about $3.00 a day now, Miss Finley," answered Mary, wondering why her employer was suddenly so curious about the milk delivery business.

Later in the day, after she had finished her work, Mary sat at the kitchen table rereading the newspaper headlines. Martha had come into the kitchen again, this time to beg some bread scraps to feed the birds.

"There's a statue of a lady coming to New York. They call it 'colossal,' " she stated emphatically. "This article says her nose is four feet long, that she weighs 225 tons, is 151 feet from head to toe, and can hold 40 people in her head!" Mary gasped in awe.

"Oh, you must be referring to the statue that France has given to the United States. It has been in the works for almost twenty years," Martha said with a chuckle.

"Well, she's finally landed," remarked Mary. "And she's called the 'Statue of Liberty.' It says she represents two things: the spirit of freedom and American's willingness to welcome people from all over the world."

"Yes, I read about it. Isn't it wonderful, Mary? The only problem now is that there is no pedestal to put her on. They are calling for gifts and donations to help build the pedestal. One account told of a poor sewing girl who sent fifty cents—all she had. It is a shame that the people who could easily afford it have not yet gotten behind this great cause," replied Martha. "I'm glad I was able to help."

* * * * * *

Tap, tap, tap went the new machine. Martha had been practicing for days. The 'new contraption', as Mary called it, was a Remington typewriter. It had been displayed at the World's Fair some years ago, and Martha had finally decided to buy one. "It will certainly make my writing go more quickly," she thought. "That is, if I can learn to hit the right keys and pick up some speed. This thing cost a fortune! Let's see," she mused, "what are the benefits of having spent all that money? Well—" she made a mental checklist:

—It will type faster than I can write.

—I will be able to sit back in my chair as I work.

—It can put a lot of words on one page.

—There won't be any ink blots all over my pages.

—Of course, it saves paper.

Tap, tap, tap. "Whoever heard of an old woman like me learning to use a contraption like this?" she thought to herself. "There's a first time for everything, I guess, but I'd better not tell anyone in the family. It will just give some of them something else to complain about." Tap, tap, tap.

After some time Martha became quite a skilled typist. Rebecca complimented her on her "nimble fingers," as she called them. Martha called it her "literary piano," after hearing that term from one of its inventors. Tap, tap, tap. The latest book was nearly finished, and the work had gone faster than ever.

The invention of the typewriter helped many women besides Martha. Like most inventions, it was the work of many minds and many hands. It opened up new careers for women, and brought remarkable changes in both the business and the social world. More and more women could earn their own living. The Young Women's Christian Association (YWCA) of New York offered typing classes which were quickly filled. Typing rapidly became one of the few occupations for women other than teaching.

"Hurry, Miss Finley," called Mary from the front hall. "Look out the window. The picture man is coming down the street. See the sign on his wagon? I'm going out to ask him to stop—you need to have your image made." Out the door she went, before Martha could object. In a few moments she returned with the traveling photographer in tow.

"Here he is, Miss Finley," Mary puffed, escorting a short, amiable individual into the library. The man removed his hat and made a low bow, taking in the room, rows of books, and the elderly lady all at a glance.

"Good day, Miss Finley. Do you wish a likeness

made? I have my view camera handy and I can have one for you in just a jiffy—for a modest fee, of course," he added with a charming smile.

Martha wasn't sure. "Go ahead," urged Mary. "I've never seen a picture of you. You owe it to your nieces and nephews, if not your many fans, to have your picture made. Please, Miss Finley."

After some further persuasion, Martha consented. She did a bit of fussing over which dress to wear and tried to smooth her hair. The photographer—one of thousands who crisscrossed America in horse-drawn wagons during this time—readied his equipment. Quick and sure in his handling of the mysterious contraption, the image was soon taken. Later, when the picture was handed to Martha, she couldn't get over the miracle of this new invention. She had Mary bring a mirror so she could compare herself with the picture. Then shaking her head in amazement, she promptly instructed Mary to place the daguerreotype on the parlor table.

The fourteenth Elsie book—*Christmas with Grandma Elsie*—came out in 1888. It was a delightful account of a real old-fashioned Christmas as Martha had celebrated it as a child many years before in South Bend, Indiana. More importantly, it emphasized the true meaning of this most special holiday.

The year also brought sadness and grief. Mrs. Finley, Martha's beloved stepmother, passed away on August 17th, about four months after Martha's sixtieth birthday. As the family was well known in the Cecil County area, many people attended the funeral. Mrs. Finley was buried in Elkton's Cemetery on Water Street. She had been the only mother Martha had ever known, and a dear friend as well.

Chapter Fourteen

THE PUBLIC WANTS TO KNOW

MARTHA'S TYPEWRITER was seldom idle. By 1889 there were fifteen books in the Elsie series, and within the next four years four more followed. Nor was she finished with the Mildred series. It was reported by some magazine articles that the Mildred books were autobiographical, because they read so much like Martha's experiences in real life, but she never confirmed or denied this. The last Mildred book—which brought the series to seven—was completed in 1894.

The famous women's magazine, the *Ladies Home Journal*, printed an article about her. The goal of its publishers was to attract one million subscribers, and in an effort to attain that goal, they began to have well-known authors contribute to the magazine's pages. Articles were also written about such famous writers as Louisa May Alcott and Mark Twain. The already high yearly rate of fifty cents per subscription was raised to one dollar.

The article about Martha read, in part:

She has kept her personality so completely hidden from a curious public that it is almost as an entire stranger to her readers that the *Ladies Home Journal* is able to present Miss Martha Finley.

The article went on to relate that Martha had been in failing health for some time, but had maintained her cheerful personality and was loved by all those who knew her. The public was told she was somewhat of a recluse, spending her leisure time with family and friends.

Martha's nephew Charles Jr. was visiting one Saturday morning. Mary had brought him a glass of milk and a plate of chocolate chip cookies fresh out of the oven, and he was happily munching away. Though he was only twelve years old, he—like the rest of his family—was an avid newspaper reader, and often discussed current events with his father. Today, the paper had contained an article about his famous aunt. Martha had already seen it, but had said nothing.

"Look," he said happily, picking up the paper, "here's a description of you, Aunt Martha. It says you are of average height, pleasingly plump (Martha smiled at this), that you have snow white hair, a large nose, and beautiful smiling eyes." He looked over at her impishly, a cookie in one hand and the paper in the other.

"Just how large do they say my nose is?" laughed his aunt.

"Here's more," the boy laughed. "According to this, your favorite colors are navy blue and grey. Even what you wear must be important to the public!" he exclaimed with satisfaction. "The article goes on to say that you are a woman of deep religious faith, and an independent thinker."

Martha was amused by all the fame and notoriety. She told her nephew that she really didn't enjoy being written about, but she supposed the statements were true.

"I do get tired of reporters wanting interviews. Some even want to come from as far away as Baltimore and Philadelphia, just to talk to me. I'd rather live a private life and be happy. God has been good to me all these years."

Young Charles looked at his aunt with awe. "It must be fun to be so famous. The boys at school ask me about you, and some of them have read *Our Fred*. They can't believe that I'm actually related to you!"

* * * * * *

One morning Mary was shuffling through an old trunk in her bedroom. Always one to keep "treasures," as she called them, she came across an old newspaper clipping about President Ulysses S. Grant's visit to Elkton a few years ago. As she scanned the article it brought back pleasant and exciting memories. Since it was almost time for lunch, she closed the old trunk, placed the clipping in her apron pocket, and went down to the kitchen.

Over lunch, Mary reminisced about the presidential visit. Pulling the clipping out, she said, "Look what I found in my trunk this morning. It's all about President Grant's visit to Elkton. He came here to see the United States postmaster general," she exclaimed as she refilled Martha's teacup. "That was the most exciting thing that ever happened in our town. Can you believe it? President Ulysses S. Grant coming to Elkton! Land sakes! I sure wanted to see him!" she chattered as she refilled the sugar bowl and smoothed the tablecloth.

"When I found out they were going to the Methodist church on Sunday, I figured the good Lord wouldn't mind if I wasn't my faithful self at my own church just that one time. And you know what,

Miss Finley, President Grant was as impressive as I had always heard. He had a white beard and mustache, and he sure did look like he could run our country's affairs."

Sipping her tea, Martha chuckled. "Why Mary, your eyes must have been as big as saucers, and you probably didn't hear a word of the sermon that morning!" Mary's eyes gleamed as she relived the scene. "And I loved ever minute of it."

Summer came and went. The leaves changed from their many shades of green to the fall hues of red and orange and yellow and gold, dropping from their branches and whirling about in the wind before they finally carpeted the lawns, the walks, and the streets of the village of Elkton. The robins and sparrows flew South, and soon snow blanketed the ground. Martha celebrated the true meaning of Christmas—just as she wrote about in The Elsie Books—with her brother Charles and his family. They had a joyous holiday.

The spring of 1894 arrived, and with it Martha's sixty-sixth birthday. She received many congratulatory notes from family, friends, and a host of admiring readers.

Spring was Martha's favorite time of year. At her request, the gardener planted pansies in the window boxes. She told the neighborhood children they were 'flowers with a face.' The children laughed and looked for the 'faces' she spoke of, but they were never quite sure they were seeing the same thing Miss Finley saw.

Wisteria, with its showy clusters of bluish-lavender blossoms, climbed the lattice of the side verandah, and gave many moments of pleasure to the two members of the household when they looked out the windows. Martha reminded the gardener to keep good wet soil there, so this heavily foliaged plant would grow rapidly.

On May 5, 1894, Elkton's *Cecil Whig* printed a lengthy article about Miss Martha Finley. They called it "A Chat with an Authoress." The article gave the history of the Finley family, as told by Martha in the interview, and gave the residents of Cecil County insight into one of their most prominent citizens. It mentioned that her favorite daily newspaper was the *Philadelphia Ledger* (the *Cecil Whig* was not a daily), and that reading it was the first thing she did each morning. She never lost her interest in current affairs and in the political world.

The *Cecil Whig* wrote: "Miss Finley in her own home is a charming hostess, and the occasion of the *Whig* representative's call upon her was one of a most cordial reception. The authoress is truly a personification of her best literary characters, and one takes his departure from her home greatly pleased, and desirous of becoming better acquainted with Miss Finley through a close study and reading of all her works . . . No authoress is more endeared to the young readers of America than Miss Martha Finley, of 'Elsie' book fame, whose handsome home on East Main Street is an example of refinement in its appointments and environments."

* * * * * *

Sundays were quiet for Martha. No longer able to attend church, she spent her day with her Bible and her religious books. Like her heroine Elsie Dinsmore, she never read the newspaper or any other secular writings on this special day of the week, believing it should be kept strictly the Lord's day.

Her routine the rest of the week was quiet as well. Martha wrote, kept up with her reading, rested when Mary insisted upon it, and spent time with the family members who visited her frequently.

One day, her doctor came for a visit. "Miss Finley, my dear," he admonished, "you simply must slow down and rest more. Your eyes are in terrible shape and stronger glasses are not available." He spoke in a gentle but firm tone. "It's time you gave up this book writing. Haven't you written enough? My word, don't you realize how much pressure it puts on you? As your doctor, I must insist that you stop writing, or at least greatly slow down your pace."

Prescribing more medicine for Martha, he left, shaking his head and muttering to himself about an old lady who simply would not give up.

Martha kept writing.

* * * * *

One day, Martha was sipping her tea and relaxing in a kitchen chair while Mary fixed lunch for the two of them.

"I heard at church that Elkton is building a reservoir just a ways down the street—just outside of town," Mary said conversationally.

"Why Mary, how nice. Our town greatly needs a storage place for large amounts of water. It could then be run through pipes into homes and businesses. In fact, the pipes could even be run into our kitchen, so that water could come out of a faucet above the sink. That would mean no more running outside to the pump to get water." With a twinkle in her eye, she said slyly, "Water could also be run to a water closet—a 'chalet de necessitate.' You know what I mean, don't you? I think a reservoir would be excellent for our town. I'm glad to hear of it, because it means that soon we will be able to have inside plumbing. I must speak to Charles about this!"

The medicine show that rolled in that summer brought much excitement to the little town. It was a furious Mary who returned from the demonstration to tell Martha all about it. She had become the eyes and ears for her employer, bringing her all the local news.

"That Jeremiah Honeycutt—he calls himself a doctor—is down on the vacant lot scaring everyone who is foolish enough to listen!" Her face red with fury, she continued, "I never heard such nonsense!"

"What is he saying? Calm yourself and tell me about it."

"Well, a man came out and described all these horrible diseases and just scared 'em good. Then Dr. Honeycutt came out, held up a bottle of greenish liquid, and guaranteed that it would cure any and every ailment. You should have seen all the people that believed all that rubbish and spent their hard-earned money on such foolishness." Mary stood with her hands on her hips, indignation written in every line of her face.

Martha chuckled. "My father said those sorts of people used colored water and sweetener to fill their bottles. How much was he charging?"

Mary fumed. "He was charging a whole dollar for it. There ought to be a law against it. He's even got a large sign on his wagon that says 'If I can't cure it, you ain't got it.' Hogwash!" she exclaimed as she huffed off to the pantry to shelve the groceries.

* * * * *

It was Friday, July 31st, 1896. Martha's telephone rang. Having had it no more than a week, she was startled at the loud ring. Thinking Mary would answer, however, she waited, but then glancing out the window, she saw her housekeeper hanging clothes on the line. Martha got up from her typewriter to answer the insistent ringing of her newest "contraption."

"The Finley residence," she announced hesitantly.

"Well, hello, my dear sister!" exclaimed Charles. "I was wondering whether anyone was home."

"Oh, hello, Charles. Yes, I'm sorry, but I was working. I thought Mary would answer it, but she is outside at the moment. And to tell you the truth," she chuckled, "I am still a bit afraid of this thing. I'm not sure which end to speak into—and the ring is so loud!"

"Well, if it's any consolation, I'm having a little trouble getting used to it also," confessed Charles. "It still amazes me that I can actually speak to you from down here at the end of Main Street." Then, changing the subject, he said, "Your name is in the *Cecil Whig* again. It seems like every time I turn around, there's something about you in the paper!" he said with a laugh.

Martha laughed, too. "What does it say this time? I haven't read it yet."

"I'll read it to you, then. It says, 'Martha Finley, well known authoress, realizing the importance of a good library in connection with the local high school, has very generously offered to donate *The International Cyclopedia*, containing fifteen volumes.' "

"Oh, yes, I had forgotten about that. I thought the young people at the school should get a new set of reference books. Up-to-date reference books are important for research, you know."

"Martha, you give away so much of what you have. You donate to so many charities and—first one thing and then another," said her brother.

"I'm just happy to be able to help others. I have not forgotten how my family took care of me before I became successful at my writing."

* * * * * *

One day the women heard the clanging bells that announced that a scissors grinder was coming down the street. Soon they heard the familiar cry, "Scissors to grind! Scissors to grind!" Martha had been sitting at her writing desk while the grinder announced his arrival, and soon she saw him advancing up the street.

Mary had been complaining for weeks about all the dull knives and scissors in the house, grumbling that none of them would 'cut hot butter.' Intent on catching him before he passed on down the street, she ran out to engage his services.

After pulling up in front of the house, he asked, "How can I suit you today, ma'am? I have all sorts of notions. I have fashionable calicoes, French collars, milk skimmers, tapes, pins, needles, brooches, and bracelets." Pointing to other items, he continued, "And here are smelling bottles, castor oil, silver spoons, pocket combs, tea-pots, green tea, song-books, thimbles, and much more. Just take a look for yourself. Here's even ague bitters, Shaker yarbs, essences, and anything else for your aches and pains. What will it be today, ma'am?"

"Wait right here, if you will," responded Mary. "I have a whole houseful of dull knives!" And she hurried up the front walk to fetch the knives.

Martha watched from the window. Mary returned with the articles in question, and the grinder began to pump the treadle on his cart to set the large grinding wheel in motion. After adjusting the faucet to make the water drip slowly against the wheel, he placed a knife against the whirling water. Soon it became razor sharp, and it wasn't long before all the utensils were ready for use again. After paying for the man's services, Mary bought a new thimble, declaring she had worn out her old one, and that everyone should have a new one when they needed it. Then she bid the man good day.

* * * * * *

A reporter from the newspaper the *Baltimore Sun* contacted Martha for an interview. On the appointed day, she put on a new grey dress with lace around the collar, and arranged her hair carefully.

The reporter arrived promptly at 2:00 p.m. Mary showed him into the library, where he found the famous authoress reading about Lewis and Clark—more research for a future book.

"Good day, Miss Finley," he said with a low bow. "I hope I am not inconveniencing you. I'm Heinrich E. Buchholz, from the *Baltimore Sun*. I've had quite a train ride, I must say!"

Martha closed her book and smiled. "I hope it was a pleasant one, Mr. Buchholz. Please have a seat."

Peering over her glasses she went on, "You're a very young man—and a newspaper reporter already! I'm on the other side of the scale—winding everything up." Martha smiled mischievously. "Now, what is it you want to know?"

"What are you reading, Miss Finley?"

"Oh, I'm reading about the Lewis and Clark expeditions. It seems incredible to think they took place almost a hundred years ago. I'm hoping to use what I learn in one of my upcoming books."

"You're planning another book, ma'am? I heard that you were under medical orders to retire from your writing!" Mr. Buchholz exclaimed, showing his surprise.

"You probably heard right, young man, but I have plans of my own. I'm not quite finished with my series," Martha replied.

After asking more questions and getting his answers, he was greatly amused when this small, frail 'snow-haired lady,' as he was to call her in his article, proceeded to show him her typewriter and demonstrate her skill on the keys. He later reported that Martha Finley considered this machine to be a most valuable possession. In one of her Mildred books, she had even written of the great benefits of the heroine's typewriter.

Mr. Buchholz, knowing he had a possibly excellent story, pressed on. "What do you do on Sundays? Do you still attend the Presbyterian church?"

Martha smiled graciously. "No, I'm sorry to say, I can no longer attend church. I'm quite homebound, you know. I spend the day quietly reading my Bible, as I believe Sunday's reading should be strictly from the Scriptures."

"Do you have many visitors?" the reporter asked, pencil in hand.

"I have a few. Many of my family live in this county. My brother and sisters, and their children, visit from time to time. Friends from the church come to call on occasion, and the minister drops in to see me about once a week. Otherwise, I live a very quiet and private life—which makes me very happy."

"About your books, Miss Finley. What are you working on now?"

"Well, I'm working on another book in the Elsie series. This one will be called *Elsie in the South*."

"And your plot for this one, ma'am?" inquired Mr. Buchholz.

Martha laughed heartily, "For that, I'm afraid you will have to read the book, young man. A good writer never gives away her story lines. But, I must say, when I first started the Elsie series I had never been below the Mason-Dixon line. Now I feel much more able to write about those lovely Southern states." Then Martha smiled mischievously, and asked her guest, "Tell me, have you ever read any of my books?"

Mr. Buchholz, caught off guard by her directness, had to admit that he had never done so, but was sure he had missed a real treat thereby.

"Yes, you have," replied Martha. "But, if my books have any value, it is all of the Lord's doing. It is He who has helped me every step of the way."

"One more question, Miss Finley, if I may," asked Mr. Buchholz. "Why do you suppose that two outstanding children's magazines of our day—*St. Nicholas* and *Youth's Companion*—have more or less ignored your literary efforts all these years?"

Shaking her head and looking out over her glasses, Martha replied, "I'm sorry, but I just do not have an answer for you. That, sir, you will have to ask them."

Indeed, it was a mystery to many why these popular youth magazines did not ever allude to the literary work of Martha Finley.

After some time, Mr. Buchholz, knowing he had plenty of material for an excellent article, thanked Martha and left to catch the train back to Baltimore. There he wrote an fine piece about his visit with one of America's most famous authors.

* * * * * *

The country's first mail-order company, Montgomery Ward, which had been founded in 1872, began advertising The Elsie Books as the "Quarter Century Edition," as it was the last part of the nineteenth century. A few years later, another mail-order house, Sears Roebuck and Company, began selling the books for 75 cents each.

One newspaper proclaimed: "The Elsie Dinsmore series now has twenty, and the author, Martha Finley, is not ready to lay aside her writing yet. There's more to come. She now has number twenty-one almost ready for publication."

A few years passed and Martha had reached her seventy-first birthday. Charles Jr. was now nineteen years old and a great help to Martha and Mary. He cleaned the gutters and made all the necessary little repairs. Of course, his aunt could well afford to pay someone to do the work, but her brother Charles felt it was good experience for his son and asked Martha to continue to give Charles Jr. the responsibility for the upkeep of the house. Twelve-year-old Emilie, Charles' second daughter, often came along to help Mary in the kitchen or work in Martha's flower garden.

July of 1899 arrived. The village of Elkton celebrated Independence Day with a parade and much flag waving. The social pages of the *Cecil Whig* announced that Elkton's world-famous authoress had had a forty-foot flagpole erected in her front yard on East Main Street.

Chapter Fifteen

Early 1900's

It was 1900. The turn of the century had arrived. The whole country celebrated the new century with fresh ideas. Ladies' fashions underwent a dramatic change. Gone were the cumbersome full skirts and hoops. A new trim look took their place. In the cities, the "Gibson Girl," who represented poise and intelligence, became the popular model for young women. Sometime later young women of Elkton were seen briskly strolling the streets in their shirtwaist blouses, cinched waists, and long smooth skirts.

America was on the go; all kinds of inventions made their appearance, as well as improvements on some old ones. People were learning about the marvelous inventions of Thomas A. Edison. The smell of oil was disappearing from homes and the flickering light of oil lamps was replaced by the glow of the incandescent lamp. The telephone was being perfected, after its invention over a decade before. The years 1890 through 1900 had been one of the greatest of all time for invention. Aluminum, zippers, cameras, bridges of steel, the shaving razor, the cash register, the Ferris wheel, the radio, and many other new things were changing the life of the common man.

Over the last few years there had been many changes in Martha's family. Along with new births, there had been the deaths of loved ones. Her sisters, Eleanor and Mary, along with her brother Samuel, had all passed away. Her sister Amy passed away at the beginning of the new century. Those remaining who were her immediate family were Elizabeth, who lived in Louisville, Kentucky; Charles, who now lived in Elkton and was an officer in the Bank of Elkton; and Theresa, who had never married, and also lived nearby.

* * * * *

At the age of seventy-two, Martha was still writing. Her twenty-fifth Elsie book, *Elsie's Young Folks in Peace and War,* was published. On and on she wrote. Frail though she was, the words continued to flow.

"What in the world is that noise?" questioned Mary, running to the window. "Land sakes! Look at that, Miss Finley! What is it?"

Martha was sitting quietly in her favorite chair by the window, resting, as she had to do so often now. She laughed at her housekeeper.

"Mary, haven't you been reading your papers? That's a horseless carriage—one of those machines Henry Ford has invented. He calls them automobiles."

"What's it doing in our town? Just listen! It is so loud I can't even think! I never——" Her words trailed off. Mary definitely did not like change.

"It's not too pretty to look at either," said Martha. "It does run, however. I judge it's going about ten miles an hour."

"Just look at those bicycle wheels! Well, I declare—" exclaimed Mary. "What is going to happen next?"

Soon the horseless carriage was out of sight, but every time Mary thought about it, she would shake her head and mutter, "Utter nonsense, I say, utter nonsense. Tin Lizzie, that's what it is, a Tin Lizzie. I don't know who would want one."

In 1895 there had been only four automobiles in the entire country. Five years later eight thousand people owned a 'horseless carriage.' A man by the name of Henry Ford had an idea to build a car—he called it the Model T Ford—so cheaply that everyone could afford one. When he had perfected his invention, he sold the cars for $850 each.

Change was definitely on its way, whether Mary liked it or not. It seemed that each newspaper brought the story of another invention. Martha enjoyed reading about them. One day she read the account of two brothers—the Wright Brothers—who had built a flying machine, and had actually gotten it off the ground.

Of course, Mary's response was, "What? Flying the sky? Now, we've got men rolling on wheels and flying like birds!" She became so exasperated that she had to sit down and fan herself.

Martha just chuckled as she peeped over her glasses at her friend.

* * * * *

Martha had just purchased an electric washing machine, another new invention. It was Monday—wash day all over town—and Mary read the directions over and over again.

With a playful tap on the new machine, she said aloud to herself, "We'll just see who gets the clothes on the line first this morning. I'll be ahead of everyone in town, even Mrs. Harkins. Some say she 'cheats,' and gets up in the middle of the night to hang her wash out, just so she can be first. I've always wondered just how she does it. Maybe what they say is true."

Martha heard all of this, and laughingly accused Mary of having an ongoing battle with the neighbor lady, over who had the first and whitest wash on the line every Monday morning. Mary had even bought some of the latest rage—the famous Larkin Ball bluing—to make her wash whiter.

The invention of the washing machine profoundly changed the life of American women. Doing laundry was considered a "woman's burden" and took up about one-third of her time. The washing machine brought to an end the time when women labored over washboards and stood over hot, steamy tubs, poking clothes with a broom handle. The lady with her clothes on the line first each Monday morning held a special status in the neighborhood—and the whiter the wash, the higher the prestige.

In the month of May, Martha's name was again mentioned in the social pages of the *Cecil Whig.* The article noted that she and her sister Theresa had taken a vacation, traveling to Atlantic City, New Jersey. And they had had a glorious time. Martha had enjoyed most of all sitting on a low bench on the boardwalk enjoying the summer sun, bedecked in her long white dress and wide-brimmed straw hat, her parasol close at hand. She and Theresa watched the passersby, remarking on this one or the other. Martha dreamed of books to come, and the people passing before her—many of whom had read her books—had no idea that the little old lady on the bench was one of America's most beloved authors.

*   *   *   *   *

Five more years passed. Martha never stopped writing. She had written twenty-eight Elsie books. In the last book in the series, *Elsie and her Namesakes,* Martha introduced new characters, theological discussions, and gave hints of personalities of children, grandchildren, and friends.

One day, the doctor made his usual visit, thinking that it would be no different from any of the others. Complaining to himself as he plodded up the walk, bag in hand, he said, "I should have more sense. I'm wasting my time. This woman hasn't listened to me in the last ten years, and it will be no different this time."

But today, Martha did listen. She was tired. Finally, after nearly fifty-two years of writing, one of America's most famous authors decided to stop. She was seventy-seven years old.

Martha's health deteriorated throughout the next year. Sometimes she would gaze fondly at her typewriter, or rub her hand over the pansies lightly embossed on her Elsie books. A faint smile would crease her lips and she would murmur, "God does care about little things."

Four more years went by. Martha, now an invalid, depended on Mary to take care of her every need. She rested much of the time and received visits only from her family and friends. In January of 1909, she became quite ill with bronchopneumonia.

On February 6th, the *Cecil Whig* reported the death of Elkton's most famous citizen. At the age of eighty, Martha died in the home she had lived in for nearly thirty-five years. She was about two months short of her eighty-first birthday. The local Presbyterian church commemorated her death with the words, "She fell sweetly asleep in Jesus." Martha was buried next to her beloved stepmother in the Finley plot in Elkton's town cemetery.

Chapter Sixteen

THE LEGACY OF MARTHA FINLEY

MARTHA'S WILL, recorded in the Cecil County court house, showed her generosity to many. She left most of her wealth to relatives, although a substantial amount was left to her faithful housekeeper. Her eight nieces and five nephews were all remembered with a monetary gift. She had recorded her will five years earlier, naming her brother Charles as executor of her estate.

The Kansas real estate and her property in Elkton, along with her shares in Cecil County businesses, she left to Charles and his heirs. She named Charles, her sister Elizabeth, her niece Catherine, and her sister Theresa, as recipients of the profits from any of her copyrights after her death. Each was to be given one-fourth of the total amount on a semi-annual basis. Her gold watch was given to her niece, Margaret. Household goods and garden tools were left to Rebecca Finley, Charles's wife. The will also stated that she was canceling all debts incurred with her by family members. On the other hand, the will seemed to reflect a sharp rejection of several family members—perhaps those who had scorned her writings.

In her lifetime, Martha Finley had written more than one hundred books and had earned nearly a quarter of million dollars. In today's money this would be approximately four and half million dollars. In her obituary it was reported that she had received $10,000 in book royalties every year for approximately twenty years.

* * * * *

"Precious in the sight of the Lord is the death of his saints" (Psalm 116:15).

At Martha Finley's death, her family inherited her monetary wealth. But something worth far more than money was also left to those who loved her. Every smile, every kind word, every prayer, every gift and good deed—all these were her legacy of love.

And the millions who have read her books have become acquainted with the beautiful, gentle soul whose sensibility was given breath throughout the pages of her stories. Her writings consciously attempt to make real to her readers the image of God as Father-protector. They overflow with the assurance of God's mercy and grace, there is no cynicism or resignation to fate found in them, no repulsive language or thought. Always they reflect a world where wholesome values and attitudes reign supreme.

Through the years, Martha's famous heroine, Elsie Dinsmore, has been both praised and criticized. Some have called her a sanctimonious prude, a pious fanatic, a goody-goody, a character whose life was unrealistic. Some newspaper editors called the character unbelievable. Others felt differently, however. A biographical sketch from *All the Happy Endings* states:

The series was admired and condemned, revered and ridiculed, recommended and respected by most eminent authorities, and more important, read by millions. With the exception of Mark Twain's Huckleberry Finn, Elsie Dinsmore is probably the best known character ever to appear in American fiction.

Martha Finley was a courageous woman who saw God in everything and stood with unswerving determination to maintain her right to be accepted as a commercial writer. However, as an article written in 1939 about the Elsie books states: "Changing times and standards have banished the Elsie Dinsmore books into obscurity." And that has been true until the very recent present. Now, the Elsie books—Martha's legacy of love—are being reprinted. More than 125 years after the first Elsie book appeared, they are once again becoming best sellers.

The End

SELECTED BIBLIOGRAPHY

Clark, Charles B. *The Eastern Shore of Maryland and Virginia.* New York: Lewis Historical Publishing, 1950.

Damase, Jacques. *Carriages.* New York: G.P. Putnam, 1968.

Estes, Glenn, ed. *American Writers for Children Before 1900.* Tennessee, University of Tennessee.

Grane, R. *A Short History of the Scottish Dress.* New York: MacMillan Publishers, 1966.

Hakim, Joy. *A History of US,* vol. 5. New York: Oxford University Press, 1994.

Johnson, George. *History of Cecil County,* Elkton, Maryland: Genealogical Publishing, 1881.

Lundardini, Christine. *What Every American Should Know about Women's History.* Holbrook, Massachusetts: Bob Adams Inc., 1994.

McCutcheon, Mark. *Everyday Life in the 1800's.* Cincinnati, Ohio: Writer's Digest Books, 1993.

Scull, W.E., copywriter. *Pleasant Hours with American Authors.* n.p., 1898.

Tarr, Laszlo. *History of the Carriage.* New York: Arco Publishing, 1969.

Worrell, Estelle Ansley, *Costumes in America,* New York: Charles Scribner Publishers, 1980.